# A Soldier's Diary

# A Soldier's Diary

A Royal Engineer During the First World War on the Western Front at Ypres, 1918

ILLUSTRATED

Ralph Scott

(Pseudonym of George Scott Anderson)

**LEONAUR**

*A Soldier's Diary*
*A Royal Engineer During the First World War on the Western Front at Ypres, 1918*
by Ralph Scott (Pseudonym of George Scott Anderson)

ILLUSTRATED

First published under the title
*A Soldier's Diary*

Leonaur is an imprint of Oakpast Ltd

Copyright in this form © 2020 Oakpast Ltd

ISBN: 978-1-78282-972-0 (hardcover)
ISBN: 978-1-78282-973-7 (softcover)

**http://www.leonaur.com**

Publisher's Notes

# Contents

To the P.B.I.

SKETCH MAP
SHOWING THE COUNTRY AROUND
YPRES
Where the events described in
the early part of the Diary took place
Railways

Vlamertinghe

Kruisstraa

Vijverhoek

Kruisstr

Dickebusch

Dickebusch

Elzenwa

Lake

YARDS   1000      500        0

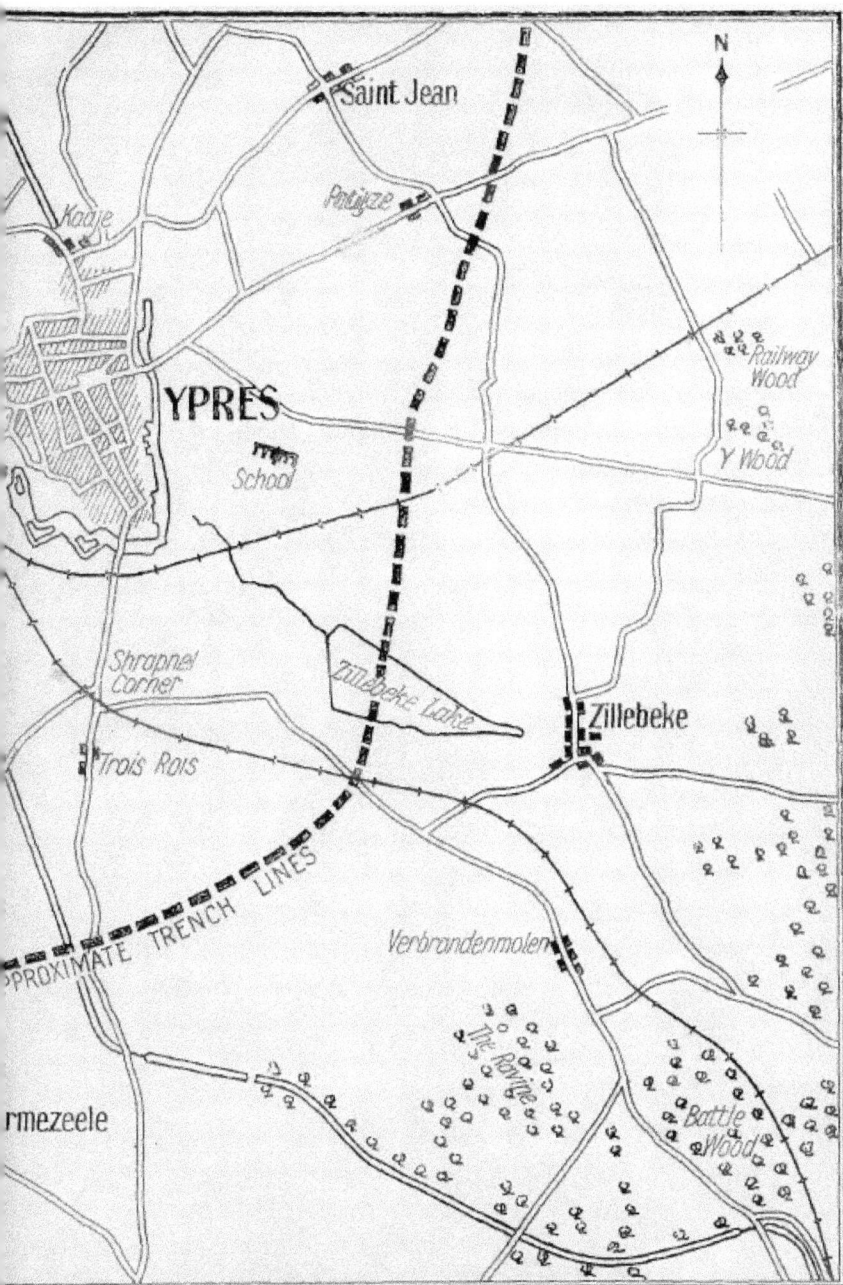

N

Saint Jean

Kaaie

Potijze

YPRES

School

Railway Wood

Y Wood

Shrapnel Corner

Zillebeke Lake

Zillebeke

Trois Rois

APPROXIMATE TRENCH LINES

Verbrandenmolen

rmezeele

The Ravine

Battle Wood

Collins Geographical Establishment. Glasgow.

2000            3000 YARDS

*Hear now a song—a song of broken interludes,*
*A song of little cunning—of a singer nothing worth,*
*Through the naked words and mean,*
*May ye see the truth between,*
*As the singer knew and touched it in the ends of all the earth!*

Rudyard Kipling,

# Preface

By Major-General Sir Frederick Maurice

Lord Robert Cecil has said that he is amazed at the false picture of war given by the history books, and that he trusts that the historians of the future will give us a better picture of what war really is than have historians of the past. I doubt if they will. They are concerned with the statesmen who direct and the generals who control, rather than with the soldier who fights, they have neither time nor space to concern themselves with the things that mattered to the men in the ranks. We can only get the things that matter, the misery, suffering, and endurance, the filth, the horror, the desolation, which are a part and the greater part even of the most triumphant progress in modern war, from the men who have experienced them. The reason for the publication of this diary is given by the author in his entry for October 6.

> The only way to stop war is to tell these facts in the school history books and cut out the rot about the gallant charges, the victorious returns, and the blushing damsels who scatter roses under the conquering heroes' feet. Every soldier knows that the re-writing of the history books would stop war more effectively than the most elaborately covenanted league which tired politico-legal minds can conceive.

Again, in the last entry of all, written after the author has been watching the Swedish Royal Troops changing guard at the palace:

> Is there no one with the courage to tell them that war is

not like this, that there will come a day without music, and no admiring eyes, but when 'the lice are in their hair and the scabs are on their tongue'? Surely our years of sacrifice were vain if the most highly educated people in Europe remain in ignorance of the real nature of war and are open scoffers at the League of Nations.

These are not the words of a conscientious objector, nor of a neurasthenic, introspective man. They are written by a keen, healthyminded, sport-loving, young Englishman, who passed through the war at the front, did his duty nobly, and behaved with great gallantry. He describes in vivid, clear language, just what he saw, he does not cover up the horrors with fine phrases, but just sets them down in their place alongside the stories of devotion and sacrifice, which make up the high lights in the picture. It is remarkable that this story, which even today makes one shiver, is not an account of the grim struggle for the defence of Ypres, of the grimmer fight through the mud to Passchendaele, nor of the great retreat when the Germans swarmed over our lines in March, 1918, but of the period when the tide had turned definitely in our favour, and our armies swept forward to final victory.

It is an account of triumphant war as seen in the front line. We are told that the public today is weary of war books. It may well be weary of war books of a certain kind, but I hope it is not weary of learning the truth about the war, and every word in this book rings true. One of the surest ways to get another war is to forget about the past war.

F. Maurice.

30th Nov., 1922.

# A Soldier's Diary

*April 23,* 1918. Arrived at the R.E. Base Depot, Rouen, and was delighted to find a pile of letters waiting for me. Damn fools that we are, we are all fretting to get back into it again—the lines must be very thin nowadays. In the evening had an excellent Mess Smoking Concert, plenty of champagne, and a terrific "fug" in the ante-room. Heaven knows when we will have another night like this as we are at the last outpost of civilisation again.

*April 24.* Wasting time all day at the Demolitions School. God! what fools we are. Up in the line men are dying like flies for lack of reinforcements—here are thousands of troops and we cannot go because the R.T.O.'s staff is too small to cope with the railway embarkation forms!

*April 25.* Several fellows posted to companies today, so that it looks as if we shall soon be over the wall that Haig spoke about and with our backs to it again.

*April 26.* More Demolitions—news still very bad—if they don't let us go to the Huns methinks they will come to us.

*April 27.* Demolitions again. We destroyed a steel rail and heard a fragment of it go humming away over our heads just like a shell. About ten minutes afterwards the colonel came down with great wind-up and chewed us all to pieces for being careless. Our piece of rail had evidently gone right over the camp and landed somewhere near the Revolver Range. Unfortunately, the colonel had heard it humming over his hut and it had nearly frightened him to death!

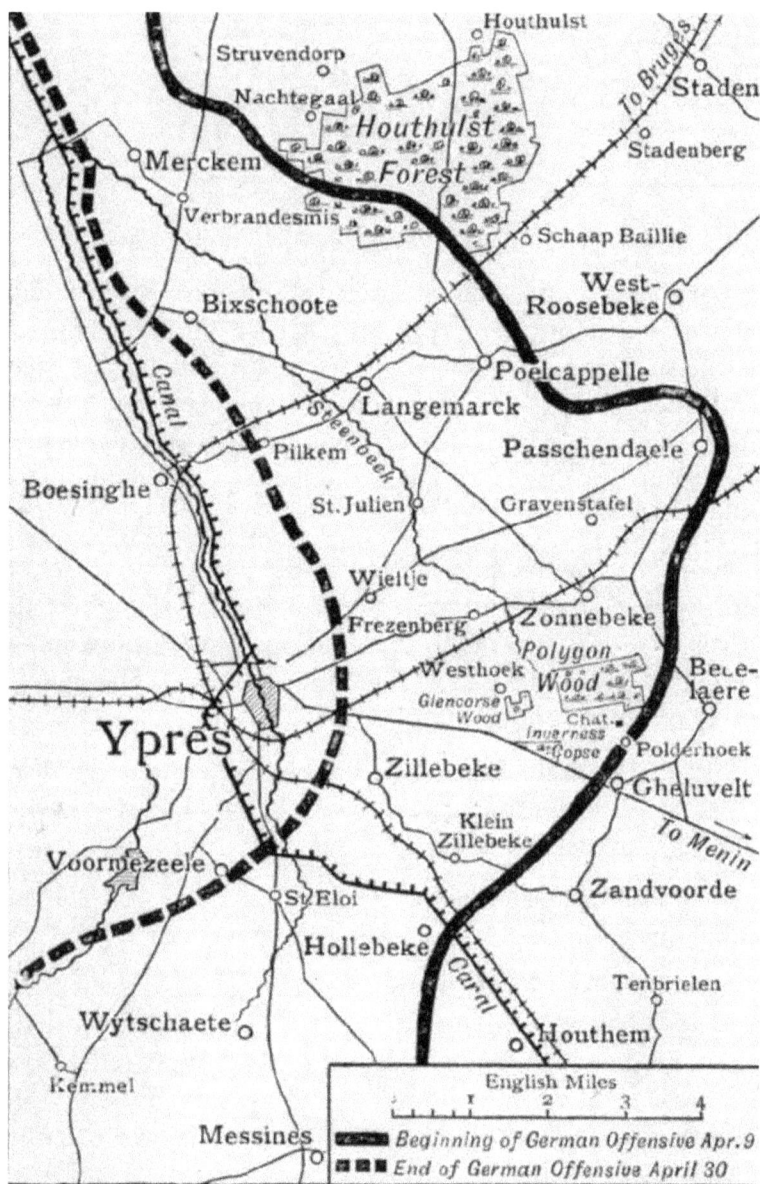

Houthulst

Struvendorp

Nachtegaal

To Bruges

Staden

Merckem

Houthulst Forest

Stadenberg

Verbrandesmis

Schaap Baillie

West-Roosebeke

Bixschoote

Poelcappelle

Steenbeek

Langemarck

Pilkem

Passchendaele

Boesinghe

St. Julien

Gravenstafel

Wieltje

Frezenberg

Zonnebeke

Polygon Wood

Westhoek

Glencorse Wood

Bece-laere

Ypres

Inverness Copse

Chat.

Polderhoek

Zillebeke

Gheluvelt

Klein Zillebeke

To Menin

Voormezeele

St Eloi

Zandvoorde

Hollebeke

Tenbrielen

Wytschaete

Canal

Houthem

Kemmel

English Miles

Messines

Beginning of German Offensive Apr. 9

End of German Offensive April 30

Canal

*April 28.* Church parade.

*April 29.* Learning how to make dug-outs as practised by an officer who has never heard a gun go off—I wonder if the Huns do silly things like this.

*April 30.* Wasting ammunition all day on the Lewis Gun Ranges.

*May 1.* Bayonet fighting—so that it looks as if we may eventually get into it again. One man down from the line today says that he has seen R.E. Field Coys. holding the front lines with P.B.I. in support. Oh! let us be joyful!

*May 2.* Had the day off as I am Orderly Officer tomorrow. Went out with Lucas and two nurses and crossed the Seine by an old-fashioned rope ferry. Climbed the hills on the far bank and spent a glorious day in the woods—scenery magnificent and everything so unlike war. In the evening we boarded a river steamer and went downstream four or five miles to Rouen. Had tea (so-called), took the nurses back to their camp, and back to ours by train. Rouen is a strange mixture—Gothic beauty and twentieth century filth!

*May 3.* Quiet day. Could hear distant gunfire in the evening—presumably at Amiens.

*May 4.* Lucas and Richards went up the line today.

*May 5.* Church parade. Wrote a lot of letters and pretended to be happy.

*May 6.* Borrowed a horse from the Cavalry Depot and went for a ride with one of the nurses. Had a ripping lunch at a little *café* in Petit Couronne—omelettes and fresh butter (to say nothing of the nurse) are much nicer than bully and dry biscuit. In the evening played the cavalry at rugger and whacked them 8-6 after an abnormally hard game. We did enjoy ourselves.

*May 7.* Lazy day! Sometimes I wonder if there really is a war on—these people here don't know about it, and in England they must naturally know less.

*May 8.* Very enjoyable ride in the Forêt de Rouvray with Major J. Had a damn good nag.

*May 9.* Poor old Jock received news of his brother's death in Mespot—knocked him up badly.

*May 10.* Great joy. I am posted at last and to my old coy.— good old war again!

*May 11.* At Last!!! Left Rouen in a crowded troop train and made myself thoroughly miserable by wondering if I should ever come back and what everybody was doing at home, etc., etc. Silly ass!

*May 12. Sunday.* Passed through Boulogne and Wimereux early in the morning and then through Calais and Cassel and on to Heidelbeck, where we slept in the train. Hun planes came over in the night and tried to bomb the train, but they didn't get anywhere near us.

*May 13.* Set off at 9 a.m. to find the company, and after walking eleven miles with my pack found them at one of the old camps in the Ypres Salient—quite like home again. The camp is surrounded by guns, and a battery of 9.2 howitzers just behind us make life unbearable. In the evening the Divisional Concert Party gave us a very good show in spite of the fact that the "theatre" was continually shaken by shell explosions.

*May 14.* Went up the line with Mellor to take over his work on the Green Support Line. Paid my respects to Ypres again—it doesn't alter much. Whilst I was writing a Bosche plane came over our camp and brought down two of our Parseval balloons in flames. All the observers managed to get into their parachutes and landed in the woods about 200 yards away. Later on two more Bosche came over, but one was driven off and the other forced to descend with a broken propeller.

*May 15.* Very heavy bombardment last night and early this morning—our own batteries replied so we had very little sleep. The hens laid five eggs. Went up to Ypres again to make some gas-proof dug-outs.

*May 16.* Working in the line all day and saw several air fights but no casualties on either side. At night went up again and had 200 P.B.I. constructing a barricade on the main Ypres-Poperinghe road. Enemy strafed the 9.2 howitzer on the Plank Road, and as we passed his shells were falling about 20 yards away from us. We didn't stay to observe his shooting, which was a little too good to be comfortable!

Arrived on the job and found that half the working party had gone astray owing to Brigade H.Q. giving wrong orders. Damned asses in their well-cut breeches—if they had to flounder about in trenches all night, they would be more careful.

The Ypres Salient on an ordinary lively night is a sight to be remembered. The rise and fall of the Verey Lights makes a circle of fire all round us, and except just where the Poperinghe road connects us with the rest of France we appear to be completely surrounded. It is more than a marvel to me how they have failed to cut us off in that little bottle-neck. On this particular night Fritz was raining shrapnel into Dickebusch and our people were giving him a warm rime in reply.

The 4.5 howitzers were firing hammer-and-tongs, and as I watched the angry shell-bursts on the ridge in front I began to feel quite sorry for the Bosche infantry. However, his field guns sent some high explosive over just to the left of my barricade, and my sympathy rapidly vanished. Cycling back in the grey of the morning we saw a 9.2 howitzer being tugged into position by a tractor and a cottage in Brandhoek just set on fire by a direct hit. We didn't linger!

*May 17.* Working on the barricade again. Much quieter night, but in the direction of Kemmel there was a very violent bombardment lasting about 20 minutes. Probably a raid by the French. At midnight went into support battalion dug-out for a whisky and whilst inside the Bosche got a direct hit on top with a gas shell. On way home noted the cottage in Brandhoek still smouldering after last night.

*May 18.* Finished the barricade except for wiring and the barrels of earth for the fairway. Also completed No.2 Post. Got

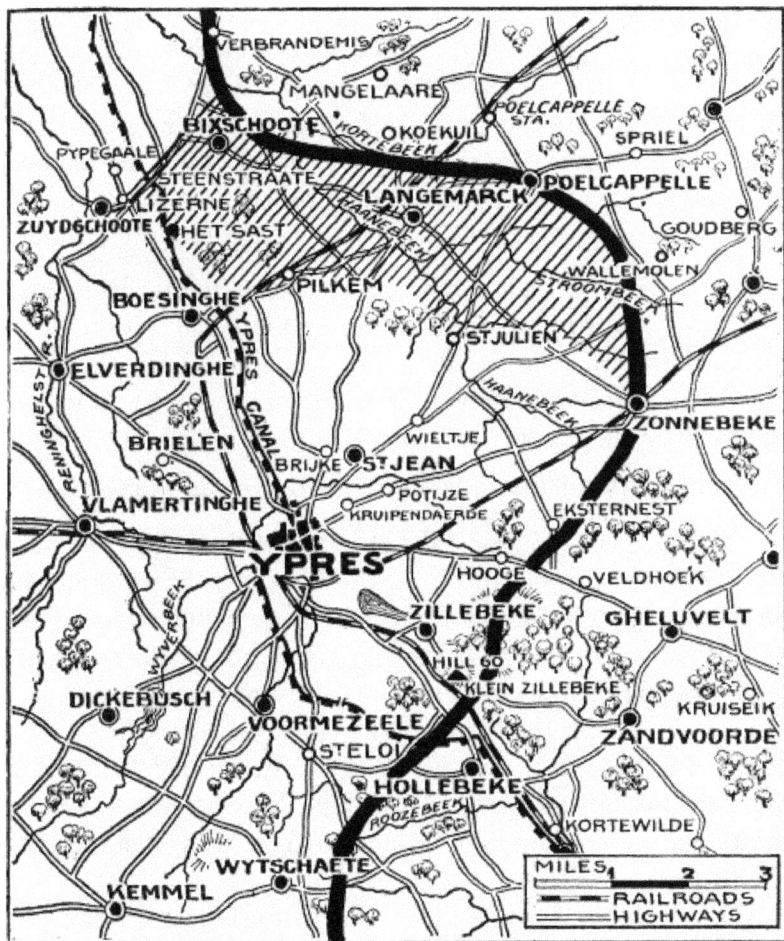

VERBRANDEMIS
MANGELAARE
POELCAPPELLE STA.
BIXSCHOOTE
OKOEKUIL
SPRIEL
PYPEGAALE
KORTEBEEK
STEENSTRAATE
POELCAPPELLE
LIZERNE
LANGEMARCK
ZUYDGCHOOTE
HET SAST
GOUDBERG
HAANEBEEK
PILKEM
WALLEMOLEN
BOESINGHE
STROOMBEEK
ST.JULIEN
ELVERDINGHE
YPRES CANAL
HAANEBEEK
RENINGHELST R.
ZONNEBEKE
WIELTJE
BRIELEN
ST.JEAN
BRIJKE
POTIJZE
VLAMERTINGHE
KRUIPENDAERDE
EKSTERNEST
YPRES
HOOGE
VELDHOEK
WYVERBEEK
ZILLEBEKE
GHELUVELT
DICKEBUSCH
HILL 60
KLEIN ZILLEBEKE
KRUISEIK
VOORMEZEELE
ZANDVOORDE
STELO
HOLLEBEKE
ROOZEBEEK
KORTEWILDE
WYTSCHAETE
KEMMEL

MILES 1 2 3
——— RAILROADS
——— HIGHWAYS

strafed by a 5.9 on the way up, and had wind vertical—10 shells all to myself and very close. Very quiet night except for a few rounds of shrapnel on the barricades.

*May 19. Sunday.* Rode round with the skipper, taking over all the demolitions from him as he goes to the gunners tomorrow as Liaison Officer. I am now responsible for the explosive charges under all the bridges behind Ypres, and in case of evacuation of the salient I've got to be the last man to leave, blowing up everything before I go. It's a regular suicide club, as I know that fully half the charges won't go off unless I fire my revolver into them—disadvantages of belonging to a corps with high ideals—"blow yourself up rather than fail to blow the bridge."

A 9.2 battery fired just as we rode past them, frightening Blacker's horse and giving him rather a bad fall. Heavy drum fire in the evening in the direction of Locre—heard later that the French got 300 prisoners. Durhams are doing a raid on our right tomorrow night.

*May 20.* Busy all day on demolitions—hot day and very quiet.

*May 21.* Vlamertinghe very heavily shelled with H.E. and shrapnel just as I was going in, Bosche got another direct hit on the old church tower and brought more masonry down into the road. Cycling along the Switch Road behind a lorry when a shell dropped into the swamp about 15 yards on my right. Tore some big holes in the lorry cover and splashed me with mud. Lucky the ground was so soft or else I should have had a little more than wind-up! At night had 260 P.B.I. working for me on the Green Line. They are the best workers we've had yet, and only came out of the line last night.

One of their officers told us a very amusing yarn of a patrol stunt which he did the other night—captured a Bosche, killed four, and got away with everything except his tin hat. Recommended for M.C. Heavy barrage, for Durham's raid started at 12 midnight and lasted for three-quarters of an hour. Bosche retaliation on our roads and forward areas.

At five minutes to twelve the moon was shining on a peace-

DURHAM LIGHT INFANTRY

ful but desolate scene; the frogs were croaking in the shell-holes, and the only signs of war were an occasional Verey light beyond Ypres and the lazy droning of a night bomber overhead. At midnight there was a crash behind us and instantly out guns let out together, surrounding us with a wall of noise and leaping, white-hot flame. The S.O.S. began to rise from the German lines and shortly afterwards the steady crashing of his shrapnel barrage was added to the din.

This went on steadily for three-quarters of an hour, while we grovelled on our stomachs in the mud, and punctually at 12.45 settled down to the usual desultory shelling. Had only one casualty in my party, but he was a nasty sight—chewed to pieces by a direct hit. On the way back Mellor and I cycled into some gas and swallowed a bit before we got our bags on—coughing and sneezing all night and had devilish headache.

Just outside Vlamertinghe we ran into a smashed ambulance and four limber mules and two drivers literally splashed about the road—our wheels were wet with warm blood. Later on, we found a saddle-horse blown in two but could not see any signs of the rider. One of the worst nights I have had since March!

*May 22.* Quiet day testing my charges on the bridges. Very hot and water unobtainable—tried thirst quenchers, which were worse than nothing. White with dust, and eyes, nose, and mouth full of it.

*May 23.* Another quiet day testing charges. Derry twice shelled off his job but had no casualties.

*May 24.* Heavy rain last night converted everywhere into a quagmire.

*May 25.* Beautiful hot day again. Completed work on demolitions and finished all preliminary testing.

*May 26.* Busy day handing over demolitions—jolly glad to be rid of them although it means front-line work instead. Very heavy shell-fire all night followed by Bosche attack, in which he captured Ridge Wood and Scottish Wood. Had seven casualties, and had to ride all the way home in gasmask. Hear that the Durhams have been very badly hit—two companies almost entirely gone.

*May 27.* Am posted as Reserve Officer to our forward company in addition to my own work. Working under the new major on Main Reserve Defences. Bosche still shelling very persistently all morning, especially found Brandhoek, where he fired a large petrol dump. Picked up some shrapnel which fell within two or three yards of me. Putting in a double machine-gun post in the top of a ruined windmill—splendid field of fire and view right away to the foot of Kemmel Hill. God help Jerry if these gunners stick it! Also constructed a very strong double post in a farm on the Switch road.

*May 28.* Up at 5.30 and working hard all day in the Green Line. Twice shelled out of the front line, and eventually had to withdraw all men to work on support. I have told Brigade Headquarters three times that it is madness to work here in daylight and that I cannot accept any responsibility for casualties— the German observation balloons can see us all the time, and we are shelled continuously. However, they don't get shelled, so it is "Carry on, the work has to be done!" The mists are the only things that save us—as soon as there is a clear day we shall be wiped out.

*May 29.* Had a whole battalion of P.B.I. working for me on Green Line—in this blasted exposed position again—it makes me feel like a High Church curate walking naked down the Strand! Shelled out of front line about 11 a.m., so left captain of the infantry in charge of parties and went personally to the general—got his authority to do exactly as I liked and got to work in front of the village after the morning mists have cleared. Someone will be wild at my going direct to the general, but I have shown him up and saved at least 50 lives—but what are 50 lives to the staff?

*May 30.* Tried the front line again, but Fritz knows we are there and shelled us out with low-bursting shrapnel—nasty stuff! After the men had withdrawn, I went back to see all clear

KEMMEL HILL

KEMMEL HILL BEFORE THE GERMANS ATTACKED

and was damn nearly hit by a whizz-bang. It burst in a pile of bricks about six paces away. I heard the explosion, and on looking up saw a column of bricks and debris just starting on its downward journey again. It rattled all over my tin hat but I was otherwise untouched. Later on, some shrapnel whizzed into the parapet at my feet and some more crashed through an old notice board by my head. Hadn't a single casualty all morning. My luck is still miraculous and it seems to extend to the men. Bosche aeroplane came over in the afternoon and brought down three of our balloons in flames.

*May 31.* Two companies of fusiliers working for me on Green Line. Misty morning, so I started in front and got on very well for several hours. About 9 a.m. a 5.9 ploughed into a breastwork that my corporal and I were standing on, explaining things to some infantry. Three men were wounded and the work wrecked, although by all the laws of reason we should all be dead. Probably owed our safety to the fact that the earth was newly placed and the shell penetrated a good distance before exploding.

After this our wire was hit and the men were getting nervous, so I withdrew to support, where we spent a fairly quiet day. Very bad news comes up from the south, and if the Bosche successes continue we expect to be attacked here.

*June 1.* Uneventful day except that there are rumours that we are going out of the line for a rest. Another huge piece of masonry was knocked off Vlam. church tower last night and buried itself several feet in the *pavé*. I should think it weighs over ten tons.

*June 2.* Sunday (I think!). Received orders to more out of the line and proceed to Army Reserve Area for a rest. Great joy, and as we are much below strength expect the test to be a long one—the men need it badly, and I suppose the Brigade Staff must get their hair cut! Company marched wearily through dear old Poperinghe and spent a quiet night beyond. All officers had feather beds although we messed in a granary.

The whole road from Pop. to Wormhoudt was lined with temporary shacks and caravans where the refugees from Ypres are living. They were a noisy, dirty crowd, and the music from the *estaminets* was simply appalling. However, combined with French beer and women, it seemed to attract Tommy.

Oh! ye women of England, could you but see your heroes now—

*Singing songs of blasphemy,*
*At whist with naked whores!*

At home it is Sunday and you are enjoying the beauties of a June evening after church. I daren't think about it, my imagination is too keen.

*June 3*. Moved off early in the morning and had a long, tiring, and dusty march, after which we entrained for our final destination. We passed through very peaceful-looking country, and although not interesting, it was like Paradise after the desolation of the Salient. From railhead we marched to our final billets and arrived there at 8.30 p.m. absolutely worn out. Like a damn fool I carried two of my fellows' packs—but it makes them love me.

*June 4*. Spent a very quiet day washing, shaving, writing letters, and generally trying to forget the war. In the afternoon I cycled alone to Cassel Hill, but it was a misty day so that I could not enjoy the view. Met a pretty little waitress at the *estaminet* on the top, where I drank a bottle of filthy wine.

*June 5*. Did a little drill, etc., just to keep the men fit, and then went for a short ride—it is good to be with our horses again.

*June 6*. Weather is very beautiful. Spent the day in meditating—how I would love some books now. Gunfire is just audible at night.

*June 7*. Appointed Lewis Gun Officer to the company and spent the day lazily, apart from giving two lectures.

*June 8*. We are going to move again, although, thank heaven, it is still westwards. At 1.30 p.m. received orders to meet Staff Captain at Brigade H.Q. at 2.15 p.m., and it is 12 miles away!!!! What would they do with bloody fools like that in business at home? And they make just the same kind of mistakes when

Fatigue Duty

lives are at stake. Set off with 12 men as billeting party, and after a very tiring ride reached the rendezvous at 6 p.m. to find the blasted captain not yet arrived. I would love to write down the men's remarks! When he turned up, he told me that our billets were a little farther on at the next village, but when I got there, I found nothing arranged. After three hours' hard work (a great strain on my French!) I had everything ready for the arrival of the company.

*M. le Maire* and the farmers were very obliging people and extremely keen to help. If anything, they were a little too hospitable, and as I was in a dickens of a hurry it was rather trying to have to stay and drink beer with 17 different farmers! About 10 p.m. Mellor arrived with the main body of cyclists, and we went to the *maire's* to eat a dry bully sandwich. The old man watched us very gravely, and when we had absorbed the bully, I poured a drink of greenish-looking water from my bottle. He made an awful face and exclaimed, "*Ah! Château de la Pompe, pas bon!*" He immediately rushed into his kitchen and brought us each a huge glass of sparkling cider, and as we drank, he roared with laughter at the recollection of his joke on Château de la Pompe. After this I went out to find the company, and met them on the far side of Brigade H.Q. about 11.30.

I shall never forget how they came back that night. They were marching with our own brigade, and long before I met them I could hear the jingling of the transport, the rhythm of their step, and occasionally catches of song floating down the valley—"Annie Laurie!" They have left more than half their pals to "sleep" in Ypres tonight, they are exhausted, limping, lousy, and white with dust, yet, thank God! the spirit is still there. The ranks kept well together, and, finished though they are, I believe they would try to struggle back tomorrow if it were necessary. I am a sentimental ass even yet, but I could have cried as I stood on the path and watched the P.B.I. go by.

Except where the fitful glare from a travelling kitchen threw them into flickering relief it was impossible to see their faces, and yet I felt I knew them—hard and scarred and ugly, brown as their rifle stocks, as a real man's face should be. And always I wonder if England understands, if England will remember! How many of the ladies whom these darling blackguards have saved would condescend to trail their dresses through the hells these boys call home? I wonder and I doubt!

*There are men in No Man's Land tonight,*
*In travail under a starless sky,*
*Men who wonder if it be right*
*That you should lie snug in your beds tonight*
*While they suffer alone—and die!*

*June 9.* Spent a very quiet day settling down and getting used to the beauty of our surroundings. We are in a charming little valley between wooded hills with a pebbly trout stream to sing us to sleep at night. It is just like Cefn on the Elwy in North Wales—a week here will do us worlds of good.

*June 10.* Sunday. Was notified that a battalion of Middlesex is coming to share our billets with us, so I rode over to see the Area Commandant and had rather a stormy interview with him. Rode over again in the afternoon to try to get some tents out of him, and again I was successful, although between him and the Brigade I made myself generally unpopular. It has been some sort of *fête* day in the village today and the Sappers had a good time helping the inhabitants to decorate their little village square—it was very charming.

*June 11.* Gave a lecture on the Lewis gun this morning—what profanity in a charming place like this!

In the evening went fishing and met an old man casting with fly and wading. I ventured on conversation and imagine my surprise when he turned out to be an Englishman—he was very reticent and I should think has a past!

*June 12.* Asked the *maire* about my Englishman. Apparently, he is a real hermit, and although he has lived in the village for twenty-three years they know nothing about him—he is a fishing maniac, and they say he spends most of his time on the river. Pity I am not a novelist—what wasted possibilities for a real thriller!

*June 13.* Starting working on the construction of a new rifle range up in the hills so that the men can keep in trim. Pleasant evening fishing.

*June 14.* Busy day on the rifle range, but knocked off work early for company inspection by the C.R.E. I think he was fairly pleased with us, and he brought a message of congratulation to us from the divisional commander for our work at Ypres.

*June 15.* Worked all morning on the rifle range with a battalion of pioneers. Progress was very slow, as we were working in solid chalk, and every piece has to be drilled off. In the afternoon went for a ride with two infantry friends over the hills towards the coast. A most perfect day, and so very easy to forget that we are engaged in war. Once we came up through dense pine forests on to the bare summit of the last ridge of hills before the coast, and to my great delight we could see the spires of Calais in the distance. Instantly I recalled Matthew Arnold's lines and felt certain that he had been on that self-same ridge when he wrote them.

> *A thousand knights have reined their steeds*
> *To watch this line of sand hills run*
> *Along the never silent Strait*
> *To Calais glittering in the sun.*

——and fifty miles away the guns!

*June 16.* Sunday. Received orders to proceed to Corps Gas School for a course of training in Anti-Gas Warfare, etc. Went with ten other officers in a lorry from Brigade H.Q., and persuaded our driver (20 *francs*) to get lost in St. Omer. We had an excellent four-course lunch in approved civilian style, and on arrival at the school at 3 p.m. well—

> *Since 'twas very clear,*
> *We drank only ginger beer;*
> *Faith, there must have been*
> *Some stingo in the ginger.*

*June 17.* Spent a quiet restful day, work starting at 9 a.m. and finishing at 4 p.m. Wrote letters in the evening and early to bed.

*June 18.* Had a very interesting day making gas attacks and committing sundry other barbarities—among them walking round a room smelling bottles and trying to identify the contents by their stinks—my nose feels as if the world were composed of one vast unmentionable stink! In the evening went for an hour's march in gasmasks—what sublime, unutterable joy to get them off again!

*June 19.* Nothing doing at the school, so we made up a party and again tasted the somewhat bitter-sweets of semi-civilisation.

*June 20.* Boring day—fed up.

*June 21.* Manufacturing stinks all day—will be heartily glad to see the company again.

*June 22.* Examinations and end of the course—thank God! Felt rotten in the afternoon and went to bed—pray it isn't Spanish 'flu, as there is a terrible lot about. Shortly after midnight a party came into our hut and took out Captain Sparks and threw him in the pond. Served him right; I never knew a more bombastic idiot.

*June 23.* Went back to the company in a motor lorry, arriving 3 p.m. Found the others playing badminton over a wire net and in field boots! Still jolly feverish but cheered up to be with the company again.

*June 24.* There are rumours about today that we are going still farther away from the war in order to be trained as "storm troops"—apparently we are considered a good division and we are picked for the Grand Forlorn Hope of the Allies. Even the most pale-faced pacifist could hardly help feeling a thrill of pride when he learns that he is picked for such a venture. Myself I am delighted—until I think of the married men. It is at least certain that I am far too sentimental to be a staff officer—a man who unconsciously visualises the widows and the orphans could never do it, and to me it will always be something more than a game of chess. But perhaps that is only the natural attitude of the pawn!

*June 25.* Orders came through last night that we are moving again today, but it is to be eastwards this time. Up all night in consequence, and had company on the road with all transport by 8.30 a.m. Marching all day, *via* Watten to St. Omer, where we arrived at 6 p.m.—very weary. Had only three hours' sleep and was roused by orderly corporal at 1 a.m.—

*June 26.*—with instructions to meet staff captain fifteen miles away at 7 a.m. What a life! From brigade went forward on bicycle and arranged billets for company, which arrived at 4 p.m. Very poor accommodation and officers had to sleep in tents.

*June 27.* Spent a quiet day resting and cleaning up after our travels. Learnt that we are going into the line again south of Ypres, in the neighbourhood of the Kemmel front.

*June 28.* Two officers went forward to the line to take over our work from the French. Spent the day inspecting all our gear and cleaning guns and ammunition. We are beginning to lose our ragamuffin appearance and look something like soldiers again today. It is wonderful the way the men can pull themselves together after the times they have had.

*June 29.* All details completed and we are ready—for what?

*June 30.* Sunday. At 2 p.m. we left our billets and should be in the line about 6 p.m. When we set out the company looked smarter than I have ever seen it, the men fit and well and marching like the Guards, the horses fat and frisky, and the wagons and the harness shining like a Dress Parade. The major was away in front with Derry so that I was in command. I felt sad as I rode round the ranks for the last time and took my station at the head of the column. Then, turning in my saddle, I gave the words, and as the lead chains tightened and the pontoons lumbered slowly forward my sadness changed to pride—for the first time in my life I was leading 250 magnificent men towards a battle, and I prayed that I might never let them down.

Proceeded to Divisional H.Q. Area, where we installed our transport with the exception of the limbers. The sections then went forward to billets under the shadow of Kemmel, where we arrived about 7 p.m. Everyone very tired as it has been a broiling day and we are white with dust. Our area does not seem to have been shelled very much, and the farms and cottages where the men are billeted are almost intact. We are, however, completely overlooked from Kemmel Hill and cannot move about in daylight. The tool-carts were brought up and camouflaged after dark, and when all was settled and the men had had a meal, I went to investigate my billet.

It is a small room 10 feet by 6 feet and, with the exception of a similar room adjoining it, is the only remaining part of what has been a decent cottage. The walls were papered with newspapers printed in five different languages, and the general filth of the place was beyond description. Following my usual practice, I put Marjorie's large photograph in my map case and hung it on the wall, after which the place looked a little more cheerful. However, the guns were very active, the lice were even more so, and not even the comfort of her photograph could induce me to fall asleep.

*July 1*. Got up about 11 a.m. and spent the day until 4 p.m. lying in the sun and listening to the Decca—and the guns! The last of the French officers left us today after marking on our map where two women are to be found on the Steenvorde road. Thank God we are not like that! About 4.30 p.m. all officers cycled forward to inspect work. Everything is utterly destroyed, and the once prosperous little town in front of us is now nothing but a pile of bricks. It requires large parties of men working all night to keep one road clear for the transport. When one considers that the town has been utterly wiped out in two months one can form some conception of the intensity of the German shell-fire.

After struggling through the debris, we left out cycles behind a hillock, entered a trench, and walked round to the front. Away on the left we could distinguish the ruins of Ypres shining faintly in the evening sun, and smoking under a desultory bombardment. Closer to us was the brick pile and swamp once known as Dickebusch, and in front, a few hundred yards away, the bulk of Kemmel Hill towered above us. Two months ago, I saw it covered with beautiful woods and peaceful rest camps; now it is a bare, brown pile of earth, and only a few shattered tree-stumps in the shell-holes remain to mock the memory of its verdant beauty. The whole of Kemmel Hill and the valley and the ravines in front are one solid mass of shell-holes.

The earth has been turned and turned again by shell-fire, and the holes lie so close together that they are not distinguishable as such. The ground in many places is paved with shrapnel balls and jagged lumps of steel—in ten square yards you could pick up several hundredweight. There was a magnificent view of all the Bosche forward lines, but of course he has a much better view of ours and also of our back areas.

They say it is death to move a finger in front of the hill and all our work will have to be done at night. On our way back we carne across an old French battery position which had apparently been defended to the end in the great struggle. The guns were right in the open and must have caught the full blast of the German fire, for the limbers were all shattered to pieces and many of them were turned over into the shell-holes.

The gunners were killed to a man round their pieces, and could have no finer monument than their pile of empty shell-cases. Their bodies still lay there unburied, mixed up with the carcasses of the horses with which they had tried to get the guns away at the last moment—some were headless, limbless, and with their entrails strewn around them—most had had the clothing blown from their bodies, and some had been half eaten by the rats. A noble end and yet—how infinitely better if such true nobility could have served a better cause—or must we, in despair, admit our civilisation to be a sham and war the only reality which can show us at our best?

If any man had the power to picture the fearful indescribability of that scene, I vow there would be no war—but it is not to be—the world is so utterly detached from all this blood and carnage, it doesn't worry them, and besides, they must have recreation, "the strain is so terrible, you know." They can hardly stand it, poor things—and besides, the air raids—terrible! Mean-

KEMMEL RIDGE

GERMAN DEAD AT KEMMEL RIDGE

time we die—without recreation. *"Father, forgive them, for they know not what they do."*

*July 2.* Before turning in last night I spent some time over my maps and have now got a pretty clear idea of the hopelessness of our position. There are no trenches, but we hold a broken line of outposts about five hundred yards in front of an old main road which we are defending. The key of our position is one solitary hill, a small symmetrical hump not more than 100 feet high and entirely overlooked by Mont Kemmel, which is ten times higher. And yet the whole line in Northern France, and perhaps the result of the war, depends on our holding this little hill. Between it and the coast the country is as flat as a pancake, and if we lose the hill, we lose Calais and the Belgian ports—so much for the country, now for the men.

We have a division which, with the exception of the few days' recent rest, has had about six months of continuous hard fighting. Our front is twice as long as it should be, we are still below half strength, and most of our effectives are boys of 18-19 going into the line for the first time. On the other hand, the Huns hold very superior positions and they are flushed with victory. Such is our problem; the answer will be written in blood around the slopes of Kemmel. I forgot to say that there are no reserves between ourselves and Calais. Let us pray!

*July 3.* Went forward at 3 a.m. with the major in the hope of laying out new trenches for tonight's work. Unfortunately, the mists cleared away very early and we were not able to do very much. Fritz was apparently very sleepy and we didn't get sniped—nevertheless I was jolly glad to get into a trench again. I cycled back and spent the morning at the Dump and in looking for material. In the afternoon went forward again with my sergeant to show him the work, but was not able to do much as the snipers were very active.

Went forward again in the evening—did another reconnaissance and got a party of about 30 men out on the job by 11 p.m. We were trying to put a belt of wire across the end of a valley which offers a covered advance to Huns. Progress was very slow owing to persistent enemy machine-gun fire and horrible condition of the valley bottom. Fritz had apparently brought a gun forward specially to shoot up the gully and we had to spend most of the night on our stomachs. In addition, the transport got lost and we were held up for lack of material.

*July 4.* Got back to billets about 5 a.m., having been on my feet twenty-six hours. Had a few hours' sleep and went forward again with ten men, showing them the tracks, etc., so that they will be available as guides. Went forward again at 8 p.m. and after a terrific struggle got two pontoons of material behind the hill by 11 p.m. On way up an 8-in. shell landed between the wagons and knocked out two men whom we left with R.A.M.C. The horses were terrified, and in trying to hold them Baker was knocked down by one and badly kicked. I wanted him to go back, but he insisted in carrying on. There was heavy shell-fire all the way up and I was damn glad to get them all under cover.

Work on the valley was again very slow, owing to heavy machine-gun fire and lack of carrying-parties. Jumping down into a shell-hole when the fire was rather hot, I caught on some wire and ripped my leg, and also cut my left breeches leg right off. When the men had gone back, I tried to do some more taping out before the mists cleared but could hardly drag myself along and nearly fell asleep in No Man's Land.

*July 5.* Got back to billets to find that Derry had gone sick. More work for the rest of us, and we are nearly tired out now. In the evening Blacker crocked up and went sick too—pure undiluted funk on his part. Three officers left now to do the work of ten and the major will go soon. He hasn't been to bed for a week, and must have walked at least twenty-five miles every day. I had a talk with him and persuaded him to order the T.O. up from the horse lines, so that will make four of us. I have got two brigades to look after now. Forward again about 7 p.m. and nearly completed wire across the valley in spite of usual machine-gun fire—two men hit in my party. Heavy shell-fire all night.

*July 6.* Coming home about 4 a.m. I met the major alone,

and although nearly finished I went back to help him to lay out a new line. Poor old major is nearly done, but he will drop before he gives in. I hope we can last until some more officers come, but my eyes are jumping and my head sings like a tornado—how few people must know what it is like to be really exhausted in the body and yet to have a mind which drives you on.

> *To make your heart and nerve and sinew*
> *Still serve your turn long after they are gone,*
> *And so, hold on when there is nothing in you*
> *Except the Will which says to them, 'Hold on.'*

I hope we can.

*July 7.* Beginning to get used to feeling tired and think we can stick it now. We are all jumpy and are too far gone to talk or read the paper—the Decca hasn't been touched for days. Had another cruel night, and was on the go for twelve hours. Finished wire across the valley and got well on with digging reserve trenches and wiring reserve line.

*July 8.* Had three hours' sleep and went up again at night after a heavy afternoon's work. Very heavy thunderstorms all night made it almost impossible to move about. Was so exhausted with falling into shell-holes that I started to crawl about on my hands and knees in the mud—once I almost cried with sheer weakness. On way home I fell off my bike and was so weak I had to leave it in a shell-hole. Once or twice I touched my revolver—there is always that. It is a terrible thought, and even now, half an hour afterwards, I can't understand it—how much less can people at home!

*July 9.* Slept a bit, worked all afternoon, and up again at night. Heavily shelled on way up but no casualties. Completed first wiring of left Brigade front and most of their digging. Did an early morning reconnaissance with major and brigade-major, having been on the go fifteen hours. I think we can keep it up indefinitely now, but where our strength comes from I don't know—at least eighteen hours per day.

*July 10.* Usual sort of day. Had to walk all the way to line and back as it was impossible to get a bike through the mud. Wretched night, with pouring rain and howling wind—two poor devils killed.

*July 11.* Usual day—started clearing New Wood for digging tomorrow night. Whole area heavily shelled. Could sleep forever and would dearly love to die.

*July 12.* Went up in the afternoon to take over two more jobs—making a new roof for left Brigade H.Q.'s and tunnelling an underground First-Aid Post for the Middlesex. Had tea with the brigadier and then dinner with the C.O. front line battalion. It is really very amusing the way in which some of these old-time regulars endeavour to preserve their mess formalities. The dug-out couldn't have been more than 12 feet square, and yet they managed to produce quite a respectable four-course dinner for seven officers. It was handed on to the table by a perspiring orderly, who crouched in the entrance to a tunnel which could not have exceeded 3 ft. by 4 ft.

How the food was cooked I could never imagine, but the smells of cooking leaked out from behind the orderly, and somewhere in the depths of the blackness behind him there was a voice that swore, mightily and frequently. I judged that the Voice had produced the meal and also that it had been a hot job. Most of the soup got spilt before it left the end of the cavern, but the smell was excellent and gave us quite an appetite for the tinned salmon which followed. This had been brought up with ammunition and a bottle of execrable French vinegar from division that very afternoon.

The next course was excellent. Roast mutton, procured as the result of dark dealings with the A.S.C., fresh peas from heavens knows where, and lastly some sauce made from mint which they said had been growing last night in No Man's Land. The sweet was a treacle pudding. We drank thin whiskies and sodas which were distinctly lukewarm in spite of all the doctor's efforts to keep the stuff cool. All things considered, a very enjoyable meal and a great credit to the Voice. Did a hard night's work and got back, feeling as if I could sleep for ever, about 5 a.m.

*July 13.* Was up again about 10 a.m. and inspected explosives before lunch. Then up the line again to start another mining job—"B" Company, H.Q. Front Line Battalion. Have now got two big mining jobs in hand and the colonel absolutely refuses to send me any timber. He says there is plenty to be salved. True, O king! but to call it firewood would be flattery. However, it doesn't matter—if the whole damn shaft falls in and kills twenty men there are plenty more in England. Life is much cheaper than timber! Managed to get home for tea and dinner, but back out again all night.

While talking to one of the working-party officers a piece of whizz-bang landed between us and another one smashed his respirator. I am sure someone is going to be killed in the mines—the earth runs like quicksand, and even with decent frames it would be a dangerous job. Without, it is sheer suicide, and a shell anywhere near us on the surface will cave the whole thing in. Fortunately, the men don't realise these things, lucky beggars.

*July 14.* Informed that the division on our right are doing a raid tonight, but working parties are to go out as usual! If I were sentimental, I should have to write a last letter home every night—then I would certainly be killed. Started work on a strong point in front of the hill, and shortly afterwards our barrage started in conjunction with the raid. It was very fierce, and the S.O.S. lights went up at once over the German lines. We were watching the pretty colours when their protective barrage came down, just like a sudden thunderstorm, and I realised to my horror that we were working dead on their barrage line.

Before I saw exactly what had happened two men were knocked to pieces and the remainder were running all over the place looking for cover. There were the ruins of a farm on our left, and I was trying to get the men together into the holes around this. We got about fifteen into this and several wounded, and then they shortened range.

A salvo came bang on top of us, there was a great lurid flash and a roar by my feet and I thought I was done for. I went clean off my feet and was blown several yards, but got up and found I was untouched but nearly blind and awfully dizzy. I heard someone calling, and found McDougall. He had been knocked over by the same shell and was quite blind. We crawled into a hole together and waited to get our breath. The shells were coming just round us in solid masses so close that we could feel the earth heaving, and once or twice we were half buried. I had lost my bearings completely, and McDougall was still blind and apparently dazed, for he wouldn't answer when I shouted in his ear.

Then I felt alone and I thought I would go mad—there were rats in the same hole with us, screaming with terror, and all the time those blasted shells, *crash, crash, crash*. I felt I must do something, so I looked over into the next shell-hole and saw that it was part of an old trench. I shoved McDougall over and together we flopped down into it and felt much safer, as it was deeper than the one we had left. Then I started to crawl along the trench, and to my great delight we found some of the men.

For three-quarters of an hour we lay in that ditch with the earth jumping and falling all round us—at times the whole trench seemed to more three or four feet. A ration party out on the mule track hadn't got such good cover, and we could hear the poor devils moaning and screaming as some of the others tried to drag them back to the aid post. Some of the kids in our trench began to cry, and I felt like it myself. We were all choking, and the valley was so full of smoke and dust that I couldn't even see the Verey lights which were less than 300 yards away—only the great red splashes of fire where the shells burst.

It seemed to last for hours; the steady crashing of the bursts, the whine of the flying pieces and all around the screaming of shattered men who had once been strong. And then the smell which, if a man has known it once, will haunt him to the end of time, the most sickly nauseating stench in the world—the combined smell of moist earth, high explosive, and warm human blood.

God, in Thy mercy, let me never again hear anyone speak of the Glory of War!

About 1.30 the noise stopped almost as suddenly as it had begun, but he put down two more barrages, one at 2.0 a.m. and one at 2.30. Had an awful headache when I got to bed.

*July 15.* McDougall gone down with shell-shock and blindness, but I managed to turn out, although very sore and stiff—that shell must have been mighty close, and everyone is agreed we should be dead. Dinner with the colonel again and promised to repair his dug-out, which got badly smashed up last night. Desultory shelling all night but comparatively quiet—my head feels like a concertina and if we had more officers I would certainly go to hospital. However—

*July 16.* All my men were sent back to the Reserve line today for a rest, but as we are so short of officers there is no rest for me. In fact, the work is rather more, and I had a very heavy time explaining things to the new sergeants.

Machine-gun bullet hit a stump about a yard in front of me and drove a lot of dirt and splinters into my face.

I am worn out.

*July 17.* Was coming home this morning about 5 a.m. very weary, when Jerry put down still another barrage. There were no trenches handy and I spent a nasty half-hour in a ditch on the side of the track. When you have once been strong it is awful to lie in a ditch and quiver like a jelly when shells are falling fifty yards away. I am going all to pieces and my imagination is killing me. Last night I was alone inspecting the wire when for some hellish reason I saw a picture of myself disabled by a bullet and lying for hours until I bled to death—days it would have been, for my vitality is tremendous. For several minutes I couldn't move, covered with a clammy sweat and paralysed with fear.

Great wind-up today—the Huns are expected to make their last effort for Calais tomorrow. Every available man working on battle positions, and all guns fired a counter preparation on German roads. If they *do* attack seriously it will be the end of my diary.

*July 18.* Worked like devils all last night and then spent an awful hour before dawn, standing to and waiting for the attack.

Every time an odd shell came over, we held our breath and waited for the crash of the general bombardment. The strain was terrific and my stomach felt as if I had eaten a whole live jellyfish. The attack didn't come—24 hours' reprieve!

*July 19*. Another day of feverish activity, work, and strain. I have been thinking of Piccadilly Circus and wonder if they realise how very near they are to the end. Reconnoitred an old farm with a view to erecting a Brigade H.Q. there in event of retreat to Reserve Line. Why, Heaven knows, as if they *do* attack there will be no one to retreat—except, of course, the Brigade H.Q. with their trouser-presses, etc. Derry came back to us and is going to take over this work. Did very well in the line at night, and completed wire to Right Brigade in spite of heavy shell-fire.

*July 20*. Words fail me—a new officer has arrived and I am going to have a rest, at least a comparative one, on the Reserve Line. After starting the parties, I spent the night advising the P.B.I. on trench drainage and got soaked up to the waist. Got three hours' sleep in my soaking clothes as German attack is still expected. I wish it would come—the strain of waiting is terrible.

*July 21*. Life is getting quite enjoyable again. Spent the night handing over to new officer. The company has received four more Lewis guns which, I think, shows better than any words how well we did in the retreat.

*July 22*. Filthy wet day, spent in taking over Reserve Line from T.O., who returns to Horse Lines. The threat of attack still hangs over us in a state of suspended animation.

*July 23*. Poured all day; soaked and fed up.

*July 24*. Day goes on leave, so I took over his work in the line, chiefly concrete pill-boxes. Thus, ends my rest. Blessed is he that expecteth nothing, for he shall not be disappointed. Did a good night's work under a beautiful moon and met the major in the morning before dawn to reconnoitre some wire.

*July 25*. Derry went sick again, so we are now as badly off as ever. Doing four men's work and had a very rushed day. Why the *devil* don't they send us reinforcements?

*July 26.* Four hours' sleep and off up the line again—the first Americans came within a few miles of the line today. I think we have just about weathered the storm without them.

*July 27.* Four hours' sleep, then spent the morning on Brigade H.Q., afternoon on the Reserve Line, paid the company, and spent all night on wiring and completion of No.1 Pill-box.

*July 28.* Our sister company went over last night to destroy wire for a raid. They collared two Huns, so that the real raid never came off and was unnecessary. Good work.

*July 29.* Completed No. 2 Pill-box. Work well on with Brigade H.Q. and put up 300 yards of wire at Reserve Line. Two of our drivers and three of the best horses were killed last night. It is difficult to make comparisons where all men are so wonderful, but as an example of the purest form of stolid courage I think the limber driver is unique. In a place like this there is never more than one decent road, and in consequence it is packed from dusk to dawn with every conceivable form of wheeled transport. Food, water, ammunition, guns, wire, and everything else which the linesman needs, must pass along this solitary lane, and the German knows it.

The shell-fire is seldom heavy, as the line knows it, but it is persistent, wearing, and of the most deadly accuracy. A very favourite trick is to shell some point on the road and thus compel traffic to wait. In five minutes, they know that there will be a solid column of wagons on the far side of the block, and then they lengthen range—preferably with shrapnel. Then it is like all hell let loose. Half a dozen shells among those crowded limbers can do the most terrific damage, and men and horses go down together in a welter of blood and flying red-hot steel. Mules and horses go mad, and scream and kick, the harness breaks, they climb into the limbers, ammunition explodes, and in a few seconds, there is nothing but a mass of wreckage in the ditch and the cries of wounded men and dying horses.

Go through that and worse twice a night, every night for a

month and more, and at the end when you take the reins in the evening your hand will quiver and your feet will tremble in the stirrups. And still they go without a murmur, night after night, until a merciful shell shall take them too, and they leave the saddle for ever.

Each night they see the last night's wreckage, and, if times are very bad, the unburied bodies of their one-time pals grinning at the stars until Time and the rats have done their work. And always they know their time will come, so that to me at least it is an eternal marvel how they find the strength to go. Perhaps some thought of home, some pride of England drives them on, or the memory of some dearly loved, dead officer sitting quietly on a mule among those shrieking shells and telling them not to leave their horses. But who can tell?—they do it, and England gains!

One thing is certain, they get no medals, for there are no staff officers along these howling roads at night.

*July 30.* For the first time since we have been here our billets were heavily shelled this afternoon. I had great wind up, as I was upstairs in my canvas bath and two or three splinters came through the wall. There are some Americans near us, and as this was their first touch of shell-fire it was quite amusing to see them falling over each other in their efforts to get away across the fields. Beryl, our terrier bitch, presented us with seven puppies of every breed and colour—the little harlot!

The Americans had their first night in charge of an infantry working party and I went up to their line to have a look at them. It was a pathetic sight, and when they came back in the morning, they reported being shelled off the job and that half the men's clothes were cut to pieces by shrapnel. Combination of wind up, imagination, and loose barbed wire on a dark night.

*July 31.* Put up 500 yards of wire at Reserve Line. Second party of Americans arrived. Bosche plane came over very low in the evening and spotted our billets and the guns round us. He got away through terrific machine-gun fire, but we heard later that he came down over the lines in flames—poor beggars!

*Aug. 1.* Billets shelled again, and thought we were hit several times. Another daring Bosche came over in the evening but was brought down over the lines. Our sister company pulled out of the line to prepare for an attack, so again we are doing a two-brigade front.

*Aug. 2.* Got soaked to the skin scrambling round Right Brigade trenches and was quite worn out as I had to wear my respirator, all the time—ghastly night, with continuous shell-fire and casualties all over the place.

*Aug. 3.* Had great difficulty in getting material, as they shelled our dump all night long. It is very hard to order men to go to a place when you know that it is being steadily shelled, and yet the work has to be done. So much easier for the staff, who just say, "Do it," and then leave the details and the casualties to me. At 3.30 a.m. met the major and took him round the line to see our troubles. Coming back alone—

*Aug. 4.* —over the ridge just before dawn I got dead in line with a German M.G. firing straight down the road. I don't think it was clear enough for them to see me, but the bullets whizzed past first on my left side and then on my right. I had to lie down for several minutes and watch them kicking up sparks on the road a few yards ahead—most unpleasant, and I found it another indication that my nerves are slowly giving out.

*Aug. 5.* Heavy barrage in reply to a raid by the division on our right interfered with work and caused several casualties among the carrying parties.

*Aug. 6.* The men had a night's rest, but I was out all night with two sappers laying out tapes and notice boards in preparation for the attack on the 8th. Several times we had to go well out into No Man's Land, and once I was quite lost for about half an hour.

*Aug. 7.* Was out all night trying to get some work out of the Americans, but found it a hard job as they are not yet accustomed to working under shell and machine-gun fire, and are very nervous. Among out own men I would have considered their behaviour rank mutiny, but I kept them at it until 3 a.m. and got 150 yards done. Have never been so unpopular or so violently cursed in my life before. In the course of the wire we came across a shell-hole with a mule and three rotting Frenchmen in it, and the Americans were very worried that they had not been buried! Poor devils, they have a lot to learn.

## THE MERRYWAY ATTACK

The events that follow are necessarily somewhat confused, both from their own nature and from the fact that I was not able to set them down until some ten days after they occurred. They fell out somewhat as follows:—

The Merryway had once been a decent road, but after the fighting in June there was little left but a shattered track running at right angles to the main lines of trenches. The Huns had pushed out a very considerable salient on both sides of this track, and as their ground was rather higher than ours, they were able to make life very unpleasant for everyone around them. With the threat of more German attacks still hanging over us and the men quite worn out, the Staff decided that we must keep up out morale by trying to lower that of the Huns. An attack on the Merryway Salient was decided upon as the best way of doing this.

Accordingly, one infantry brigade and one field coy. R.E. went over on the night of August 8th, and under cover of a terrific bombardment surprised the Germans and gained practically all their objectives. All was quiet for two days, the field coy. put up quantities of barbed wire and the staff went to sleep to dream of medals.

The morning of the 11th was cold and misty, and to our great consternation the Huns delivered a very heavy counter-attack. This was quite successful, and we were all driven back with the exception of one post which held out on the Merryway. Here about 30 Huns got held up against our wire and all surrendered, although most of the men wanted to shoot, because we were too weak to find an escort. However, we sent them back with two men, but seeing that our flanks were gone and how weak

47

the escort was, they strangled the two men and joined the fight.

Everything was now completely mixed up, the grey-coated figures were all around, and odd groups of men were fighting detached battles for their own skins against heavy odds. Our telephone wire was cut, and rockets were useless because of the mist; the casualties were heavy, and it looked as if the line would go. Then I saw Bradley, a fearsome sight, with a piece of his scalp hanging over his ear and his face covered with blood, trying to collect some men. I joined him, and we got a few together and went forward again. In technical language I suppose we led a charge or counter-attack, but it never struck me in that way at all, and I'm sure we had no clear idea what we intended to do. Bradley was mad, and we went at the first group of Huns we saw. There was a tussle, we killed two and the rest surrendered.

Bradley collared one of these himself, a poor miserable kid not more than twenty, and I remember the sight of him put heart into us all. In all we got forward about two hundred yards and got in touch with the Merryway post, although, of course, we were still a long way behind our original line. This restored the line a little, and instead of pushing through the gaps on either side of us the Huns hesitated a little and finally dug in about 50 yards away. All the infantry officers were killed and every one was out of touch, so that the Huns were not followed up. During the day reliefs came up, and at night brigade reported that we held a line of posts in touch with one another about half-way between our first and second positions.

I went up with a few men and some material to try to consolidate the position, but when I got to Merryway post everything was in absolute chaos and there was only a sergeant and six men in the post and absolutely at their last gasp. Apparently, they had been attacked again during the day, and had only just kept off the Huns after suffering heavy casualties from trench mortars. It was obvious the Huns thought a lot of this post, and I felt sure they would try to take us during the night. I put all my men on and tried to strengthen the place with sandbags, and made it a little deeper by lifting some bodies out of the bottom. I had 19 men with 150 rounds each and 1 Lewis gun with several thousand rounds—this I placed at the end of the trench to fire up the track.

About 11.30 we were shelled heavily without sustaining casualties, and immediately afterwards a crowd of infantry—about 100 I think—made a dash at us, chiefly down the old track. The Lewis gun opened at once, and I was terrified to find that the Huns had a gun on our flank which was shooting straight at our gun and right into the trench. The gunner was killed at once and Cox wounded, so that the gun was silent. Then the infantry sergeant took it and was shot dead immediately. I shouted to the men to keep shooting at the infantry in front and I took the Lewis gun myself and turned it round at the German gun. I waited for him to shoot, and then fired at the flash and silenced him. I noticed that the men's firing had died down, and on looking to the front I was relieved to see that the first attack was beaten off—we must have killed a lot, as they were right against the skyline—and there were a lot of them moaning about in front.

I felt certain we could hold them if we could keep their gun quiet, so for the next twenty minutes we worked like fiends to raise some protection across the open end of the trench. Then they came again in a sudden rush, but I must have damaged their gun, and without that to help them we could turn our gun right into them and easily held them off. A small party sneaked close up to us on the left away from the gun and threw some bombs right into us, blowing an infantryman to bits and wounding a sapper. Then they shelled us steadily for half an hour and got one of the look-out men in the shoulder—another rifle useless.

At this point we had our one piece of luck—found a rum jar with just enough in it to give each man a mouthful—it put new heart into us and helped us more than twenty reinforcements. Everything went quiet for a time, and in thinking things over I had an awful job to keep myself under control. The men were wonderful, but there were only 13 of us left and fully 200 Huns all round. During the lull Cox died in my arms—he was very game, but just before the end he sobbed like a child: "My wife and kiddie, oh God! sir, what's going to happen to them?—poor kid, poor kid." And so, he died.

Shortly afterwards they came at us again, and thank God none of us realised how many there were. On the right where the gun was, we held them off again, but we were hopelessly outnumbered, and a German officer and a small party actually got into our trench at the other end. I heard the row and, leaving the gun with Willis, was just in time to see a man kill the officer with his bayonet and the others cleared off again. They were very close all round us now, and as we could see nothing, I told the men to keep their ammunition and then split them up, some to shoot forward and some to shoot back. I was frightened that we should be bombed, and surely enough they started, but the throwing was rotten.

And then once more they tried us. A bomb came right in the trench and laid out two more men, splashing me with blood. We shot like fiends and the gun was nearly red-hot, but they were too many. About eight men got into the trench and then we all went mad. It would be impossible for me to give an accurate description because there was just one fierce wild tussle, they trying to get at Willis and that blessed gun and we trying to keep them off. We were too mixed to shoot; they used a sort of life-preserver and we used our bayonets taken off the rifles. A German about my own size slipped into the trench behind me and I just turned in time to duck under a swing from his preserver.

What I was doing I shall never know, but by instinct I got my left hand on his throat, and before I knew what had happened, I had got the bayonet dagger-wise a good six inches into his chest. He went down without a groan. There was no one in front of me and I turned to find a big Hun with his back to me and a life-preserver raised to hit McDonald, who had his back to the Hun, over the head.

If I had had sense, I would have stuck the bayonet into his back, but I was absolutely wild and dropped it. Before the Hun could strike, I got my hands on his throat and we fell down together. I fell underneath but got on top and pressed until I thought my fingers would break. He was terribly strong and once scratched a great piece out of my left cheek. Gradually he weakened, and I kept my fingers in his throat until he died.

Much the same thing had happened to all the other men except one, who got badly mauled about the head and died shortly afterwards. For a moment I felt we could fight the whole German Army, especially when I saw McDonald smash in a German head with the rum jar. Now the survivors were shouting for help, but that blessed Willis (ex jail-bird) was sitting with the gun out in the open, regardless of everything, swearing like hell, and none of the Huns seemed anxious to accept the invitation. We were all clean crazy, and I even had a job to keep the men in the trench.

McDonald said something about Cox's missus, and wanted to kill ten of the "bloody bastards." During the whole of that bloody night my hardest job was to restrain the men in that moment of semi-victory; for it was still two hours until dawn. Nine out of the nineteen of us were either dead or dying, and all the rest of us were damaged in some way. Throughout the whole night I had never thought of anything but death. Relief, I knew, was impossible—if we surrendered, they would kill us, and I never dreamed that we could really hold them off till dawn. Writing now, it would be easy to imagine impressions which I never really experienced, but I can safely say that throughout the whole night I calmly regarded myself as a dead man.

It seemed quite natural that I should be, and I can't remember that I had the slightest regret. It even seems now that in some queer way I was distinctly happier and more tranquil than I had ever been in my life before. I felt nobler, mightier, than any human being on earth, and death seemed welcome as the only fitting end. Recalling some of my previous entries on the subject of war, I cannot understand my feelings on this occasion and can only repeat that it was so—perhaps something of

*The stern joy which warriors feel*
*In foemen worthy of their steel.*

It was therefore almost with a feeling of annoyance, of having been cheated of something, that I saw the first streaks of grey beyond Kemmel. I thought they would still make a last effort and waited, but we shivered in vain. In the semi-light we managed to get an odd shot at some of them who had been behind us as they went round to the front—we shot two or three more this way. Then I left my sergeant in charge and went back for a crawl to see what I could find. It was almost light now, and after about half an hour I came across a picket. They firmly believed we were all dead, and said so, and once more that odd feeling of annoyance returned. I remembered that during the night I had visualised the brigade report on the whole business:

Their Lewis gun was heard firing until early in the morning but it was impossible to reach them.

However, I went back, left some fresh men in the post and brought my fellows out, leaving orders for the dead to be brought down during the day if possible. As we went back past brigade, I dropped in to report. The general had apparently been up all night and looked very worried. He insisted on seeing the men. They were lying in the mud outside, bleeding and swearing—an awful but a sublime picture. He was deeply moved, and several times under his breath I heard him say, "Marvellous, marvellous, wonderful." Afterwards, I was told that there were tears in his eyes when he went back into the dug-out. He has had an awful time, poor beggar.

*Aug. 12.* Had my face dressed and slept like a baby during the day. At night brigade reported once more that we held a line of connected posts, and again we went out to try to strengthen them. My party started to wire the Merryway post and barricade the road, and Day went forward with a party on the right. When he got forward to where our wire should have been, he found a German party well dug-in—fully 100 yards more forward than they were expected to be. They turned a gun on Day's party and threw about a dozen bombs at them but he got all his fellows back with only two casualties, and these were brought in later. On my side the covering party were so nervous as to be absolutely useless, so I sent them back, and after that my own revolver was the only cover which the men had.

I was crawling about some 50 yards in front of the party

when a light went up and I spotted three Huns crouching in a shell-hole with a machine-gun. I had no bombs, so I went back and told the infantry officer, but he wouldn't do anything. We ceased work about 25 yards away from them.

We found the mutilated body of an infantry officer who was killed on the 11th and brought it in.

On calling at H.Q. on the way back we were informed, as we now knew to our cost, that our posts were all much farther back than was at first thought, and in some places the Huns were even on the near side of our wire. But for our great good luck in getting bombed we should probably have gone out and wired between the German outposts and their main line.

I have seldom known the line to be in a more chaotic state, and I think one more attack would just about put us beyond the count. Everyone is nervous, and no one knows where anybody else is.

*Aug. 13.* Went out after dusk with an infantry subaltern to try to get in touch with a post reported to be on the left of the Merryway post. We groped about without success and eventually saw about 20 figures moving about in one of the camps behind us. They were not more than 30 yards away, so we took them for men from the post we were in search of and did not challenge. Presently they began to move away down the hedge towards the German lines, and my companion remarked that they were going a long way forward, as a German post was known to exist at the corner.

Almost immediately afterwards they began to run and disappeared into a trench about 50 yards away. Soon after this we found our own post, and they reported having no men out and having seen no one! There was only one possible conclusion— we had been in close touch with a strong German patrol which had been moving about with the greatest audacity at least 50 yards behind our lines. Very unpleasant to think about.

Then we took a few of the better men and went out on a hunt, but found nothing. It was impossible to wire because of very frequent lights and heavy machine-gun fire. On the right of the track we could find neither Huns nor our own people, and it appears that Brigade H.Q. don't really know anything about the situation at all. It *is* in a mess. About 3 a.m. the Huns put down a heavy barrage but didn't come over.

*Aug. 14.* Had a night in bed—the third in six weeks. Heard that my infantry friend was killed, just after I left, by our own shrapnel bursting short.

Hear also that I have been recommended for a D.S.O. for the scrap the other night. This is the second time, and it is now some comfort to be definitely sure that they will never give it me. I would like to get something just for my father's sake, but for myself—I should almost hate it. We are here to do a job, not to earn medals for the sake of being gushed over by silly, simpering women who could never understand. It is a hard creed and difficult to stand by at times—vanity is very strong.

The following shows roughly some of the main points in the Merryway fighting.

*Aug. 15.* Started to wire from the barricade towards the right in order to join up with Day, who was working from the other end. Got to our first post but could get no farther, as there was a strong German post across our line. Day bumped into this from the other side, and was driven off with two casualties. I was lying down listening when the Huns fired into Day and was surprised to find I was not ten yards away from them. They sent up a light, and I could see about ten of them as plainly as daylight, all looking along their rifles. I dropped a bomb into them and departed, but if we had known they were there we could have collared the whole lot.

*Aug. 16.* Was relieved at Merryway and spent the night wiring in the right sector—quite a rest cure.

*Aug. 17.* Wiring again in front of County Camp. Shelled off the job three times and had two casualties, so decided to work the wood instead—shelled again.

*Aug. 18.* Quiet night in the wood. Slowly and surely, I am breaking up, and now I am so far gone that it is too much trouble to go sick. I am just carrying on like an automaton, mechanically

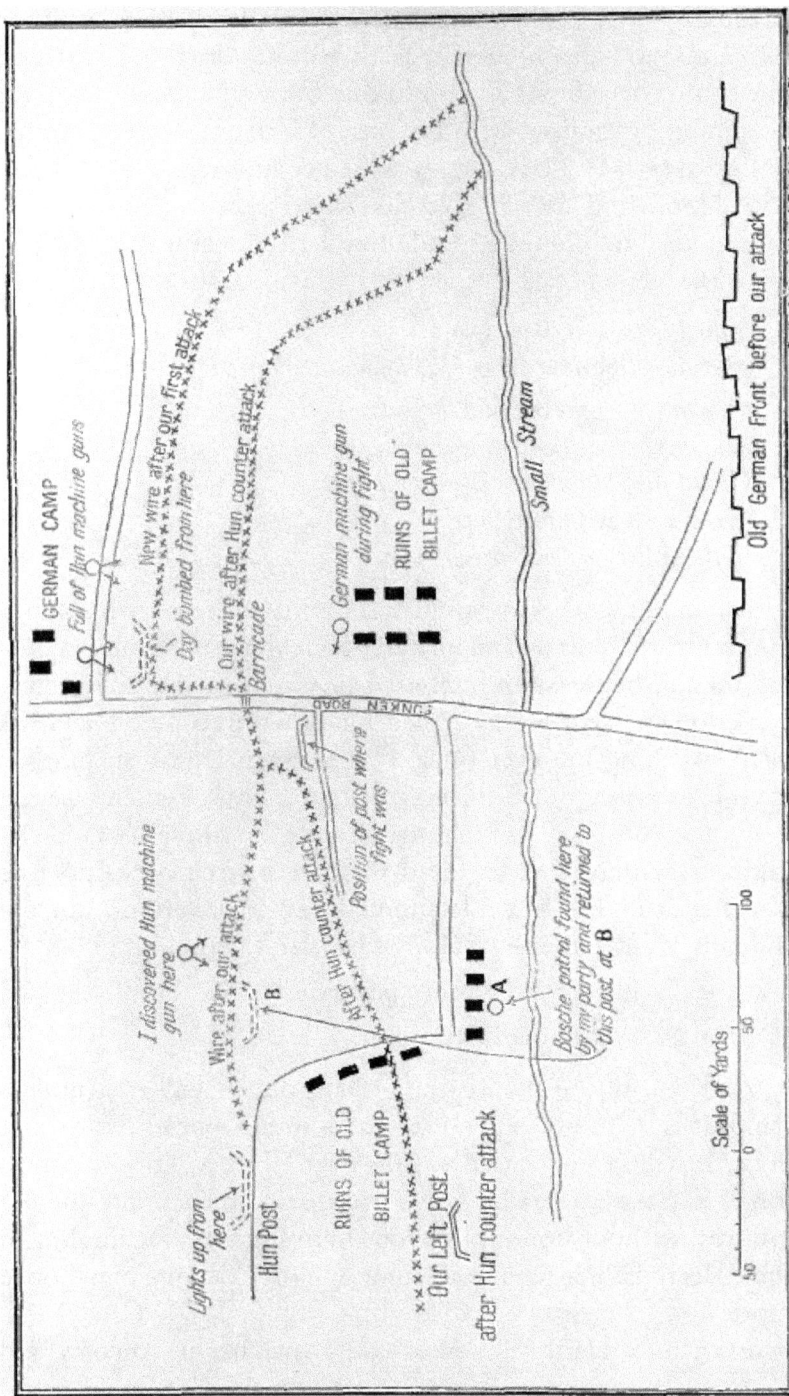

GERMAN CAMP

Full of Hun machine guns

New wire after our first attack

Day bombed from here

Our wire after Hun counter attack

Barricade

German machine gun during fight

RUINS OF OLD BILLET CAMP

Small Stream

Old German Front before our attack

SUNKEN ROAD

Position of post where fight was

I discovered Hun machine gun here

Wire after our attack

B

After Hun counter attack

A

Bosche patrol found here by my party and returned to this post at B

Lights up from here

Hun Post

RUINS OF OLD BILLET CAMP

Our Left Post after Hun counter attack

Scale of Yards

50    0    50    100

putting up wire and digging ditches while I wait, wait, wait for something to happen—relief, death, wounds, anything, anything in earth or hell to put an end to this, but preferably death. I am becoming hypnotised with the idea of Nirvana—sweet, eternal nothingness. My body crawls with lice, my rags are saturated with blood, and we all "stink like the essence of putrefaction rotting for the third time." And there are ladies at home who still call us heroes and talk of the Glory of War—Christ!

*If the lice were in their hair,*
*And the scabs were on their tongue,*
*And the rats were smiling there*
*Padding softly through the dung.*
*Would they still adjust their pince-nez*
*In the same old urbane way*
*In the gallery where the ladies go?*

Last night something went wrong in my head. A machine-gun was turned on us, and instead of ducking I remember standing up and being quite interested in watching the bullets kick sparks off the wire—Day pulled me down into a hole and has been watching me ever since. If ever again I hear anyone say anything against a man for incapacitating himself in any way to get out of this I will kill that man. Not even Almighty God can understand the effort required to force oneself back into the trenches at night—I would shoot myself if it were not for the thought of my father—O God! why won't you kill me?

*To these from birth is Belief forbidden.*
*From these till Death is Relief afar.*

And the pity of it all is this—that nobody will ever understand! It is hell to be able to see these things, but in two years I know it will all be forgotten. "It is over," they will say, "we must forget it, it was so terrible." The world will go back into the old grooves, without honour, without heroism, without ideals, and these dear, darling fellows of mine will be "factory men" once more.

Even now Hardy's sister is selling matches in Ancoats, and

my sister would refer to her as "that woman"—yet Hardy and I have saved each other's lives. And if I live, they will say "Poor old beggar, he isn't much use now, he had rather a bad time in the war," and they will pity me—once a month when I am ill. Or, worst of all, if my vitality should come back to a certain extent, I will appear quite normal and they will call me a slacker if I don't take part in games—I, who once captained one of the best rugby teams in the north! Perhaps they will even be so good as to make allowances for me!

And they will call me dull and morose and cynical—and even priggish when I keep myself aloof from them. And the ladies for whom I gave my strength and more will leave me for the healthy, bouncing beggars who stayed at home—even as nationally the Neutrals get the good things now. And there are thousands worse than I—may we all die together in one final bloody holocaust and before the Peace Bells usher in the realisation of our fears. And then, on howling winter evenings, our spirits might ride the cloud-wrack over these blood-soaked hills, shrieking and moaning with the wind, to drown the music of their dancing, so that they huddle together in terror, the empty-headed women and the weak-kneed, worn-out men as we laugh at their petty, soulless lives.

Within a week I shall be dead or mad.

*Aug. 19.* Very hot today—feeling feverish and weak—what futile words!

*Aug. 20.* Division on our right attacked and captured objectives. Three lines in the *Daily Mail* tomorrow—three hundred corpses grinning at the stars tonight—in three years oblivion—War!

*Aug. 21.* Working on Ferret Farm. On way up Fritz got six shells bang into the middle of the parties in the sunken road—one sapper and several P.B.I. hit and Day badly damaged in the face with a stone.

The limber horses behaved wonderfully, and one team didn't move an inch although a shell burst right under their tail board. Very lucky not to have had lots more casualties. On the track

The Hundred Days Offensive (8 August to 11 November 1918)

we were shelled again and had to pass through heavy gas in the region of the stream. Almost immediately after starting work Bosche put down a heavy barrage and we lay on our faces for three-quarters of an hour. Heavy shelling continued all night with a lot of machine-gun fire and gas. Was busy with casualties all night and feel like a corpse myself now.

*Aug. 22.* Beastly hot day and was tortured to death in the evening by mosquitoes—during this warm weather one usually knocks about in the daytime in one's shirt which becomes saturated with sweat, and then dries off again in the cool of the evening—the mosquitoes love the stink and after dusk they feed on us in millions—there is no respite, you grow tired of killing them and dawn finds you on the edge of insanity, swollen like a long-dead mule. It is these things which constitute the horror of war—death is nothing.

Wrote a cheerful letter home saying that I am very well and happy.

*Aug. 23.* Was riding up last night through a strafe with Day when a gas shell exploded just in front of out bicycles—we jumped off at once but before we could get our bags on, we swallowed rather a large dose—didn't worry very much and carried on with the night's work.

*Aug. 24.* In the morning bust up completely and spent the day in bed—pulled myself together and managed to get up the line again at night.

*Aug. 25.* Riding home this morning we encountered a sudden whizz-bang strafe on the road, and Day took a small fragment clean through his handle-bars—rained hard all night and practically stopped work.

*Aug. 26.* Still raining heavily, and we notice the first signs of the return of the mud era—surely, they must relieve us now if there is a man to spare in France or England—otherwise, I am afraid a week of heavy rain would clear the road to Calais. For myself, I am too far gone to pick the lice out of my shirt—I have ceased to be a man—even my simian ancestors used to remove their parasites.

*Aug. 27.* Still raining hard, but news comes through that we are going to be relieved—as I am the only officer that really knows the forward work I am to stay and hand over—only three more nights!

*Aug. 28.* Very busy day handing over all rear work to relieving company—the attached infantry parties returned to their units today.

*Aug. 29.* Company transport left at 10 a.m. for Rest Area— the Sappers marched off at 1.30 p.m. Tonight is to be my last night in the line, I hope, for a fortnight at least.

*Aug. 30.* Oddly enough, my last night was one of the most eventful spent in the sector. It was a misty night, and I was crawling about with the relieving officer to show him Day's front line Coy. H.Q., when we were shelled fairly heavily—to avoid the disturbance I made a detour of about 100 yards and got completely lost. Eventually we heard muffled voices behind us, and to my surprise, when I crawled back to investigate, I found a Hun machine-gun post with about six men in it. We avoided this and eventually struck our own line about a quarter of a mile out of our course—they handled us rather roughly in the trench as they believed us to be Bosche, particularly as my friend knew nothing about the line.

After sitting for twenty minutes with two bayonets in my ribs, Miller of the fusiliers came up and fortunately he knew me. Just managed to complete handing over before dawn and got back for breakfast with our reliefs. Left billets on horseback with Dausay as groom at 11.45. Passed through reserve billets and had an afternoon halt to water the horses in a charming meadow just beyond Cassell. We reached the company about 6 p.m. at a small village outside St. Omer—a very pleasant but a tiring ride.

Day and I are living in a large white *château*—steeped in romance from its turrets to its, no doubt, well-stocked cellars. Outside my bedroom window there is a balcony where I can sit in the evenings and watch the sun set beyond St. Omer—if only

I had my books, I might recapture myself in a fortnight here.

*Sept. 1.* Quiet day, with the usual inspections and cleaning parades. In the evening major and I rode over to take dinner with the C.R.E.—information had just come through that our outposts are on the top of Kemmel Hill. Apparently, the Huns have retreated, but it makes me damn wild to think that we should hold that blood-soaked line and wear down his resistance for other people to follow him up—I would have sold my soul to see the old division go over Kemmel, and if anyone had the right it was we.

*Sept. 2.* Went into St. Omer with Day and had tea at the club—succeeded in obtaining some butter at 15 *francs* per kilo— verily the French are a hospitable people! Returned to the mess to find the rumour about Kemmel is confirmed—apparently the Bosche are evacuating forward positions with a view to con- solidating their line for the winter. This is all very cheerful and no doubt makes good reading in the clubs at home, but unfor- tunately it necessitates our return to the line tomorrow—our test has therefore been a deal of extra trouble for nothing—two days out of the line do one more harm than good. Transport and pontoons started on their return journey tonight.

*Sept. 3.* Entrained at 8.15 a.m. and detrained at rail-head about 12 noon. Marched forward past our old billets and even- tually took over very comfortable billets from a company of American Engineers. The line seems to have gone far forward, all the old gun positions are empty and the sausages are well in front of us now.

After all, I think that the ability to park our transport in the open in full view of Kemmel will do us more good than the "rest" could ever have done. The shadow of that ghastly hill has been over us for so long that our relief at having regained it is out of all proportion to its practical value. The effect on the men has been little short of miraculous, and already they are joking about the possibilities of Christmas at home—or at the worst in Berlin! Once more we look forward to the possibili- ties of a semi-victory, and the dog-like fatalism which upheld us through the weary summer is gradually changing to something like Hope and Confidence in the Future.

But we can never again go forward with the same fiery ardour and implicit faith in the Justice of our Cause, which drove us onwards in the early days. We have seen brave Germans die with faith as great as ours, and, knowing their intelligence to be not less, we must at least doubt the validity of our first conclusions. Now we are infinitely wiser men, growing sadder as the cold light of reason destroys out early phantoms of enthusiasm. Already "the bones about the way" are far too numerous to justify the best of possible results and—there will be more before the end. But these reflections are morbid and unbecoming in a soldier—tomorrow I must inspect rifles with enthusiasm.

*Sept. 4.* Day and I working all day on our dug-out and in making a place where we can have a bath—I shudder when I try to recall my last one.

*Sept. 5.* Up at 2 a.m. and working until 10 with the whole company endeavouring to construct a road across a semi-dry lake. It is obviously a staff project and would have been condemned by a first year civil-engineering student—we cast our brick upon the waters in the vain hope that it will return after many days.

Meanwhile the advance creeps forward across the swamps in front and shows signs of being bogged as the resistance stiffens. Yesterday our two line brigades had 500 casualties, and after gaining the summit of Messines Ridge they had to fall back owing to lack of support. Thus, it seems that we shall play the German game once more by following them into the worst of the mud for the winter—God help us if we do, the 19-year olds would die like flies in a hard winter.

Had my bath and feel like a new man

*Sept. 6.* Dumped a few more tons of brick into the lake—at least it is a peaceful job and keeps the men out of mischief. Played badminton and wrote letters—the war seems to have fallen into abeyance.

MESSINES RIDGE

*Sept. 7.* Heavy gas-shelling on the lake this morning robbed us of our constitutional and forced an early return.

After dinner we turned out with torches and heavy sticks to hunt rats round the dug-outs. There were no casualties among the rats, but Day sprained an ankle.

*Sept. 8.* Still brick dumping, although no progress is apparent as yet. During the morning I walked across the dyke to talk to the company working in the morass on the far side and sincerely wished I hadn't. They had been finding bodies all morning, not more than a month dead and just coming to the worst stages. Whilst I was there, they picked up two kilted officers—glorious big men they must have been but looking so childishly pathetic as they lay there. Unconsciously we all fell silent, and I saw a D.C.M. sergeant-major with tears in his eyes. Hurriedly I turned away and, walking back to the men, thanked God that people at home can never even imagine the deaths their men are called upon to die.

We are going into the war again tomorrow. The rains are with us.

*Sept. 9.* Two sections moved into forward billets at Negro Farm—an appalling place consisting of two stinking dug-outs under the ruins of the former homestead—it beggars description but closely resembles that famous Bairnsfather drawing, "We are staying at a farm." It has poured all day, and when we arrived about eleven this morning there wasn't shelter for a quarter of the men and none for the horses. I explored two or three ruins in the neighbourhood, but they were all worse than our own midden, so we had to make the best of it. Fortunately, the cheerfulness of the men seems to increase with their misfortunes and they are now all under cover of some sort—even the horses are more or less protected from the worst of the weather.

My home consists of three battered sheets of corrugated iron, a wagon cover, and the back of a hen shed, reared miraculously against a bank of earth which is the mainstay of the edifice. Light from a candle in a port bottle, no H. and C. or modern conveniences of any sort. It is cold, damp, miserable, and the

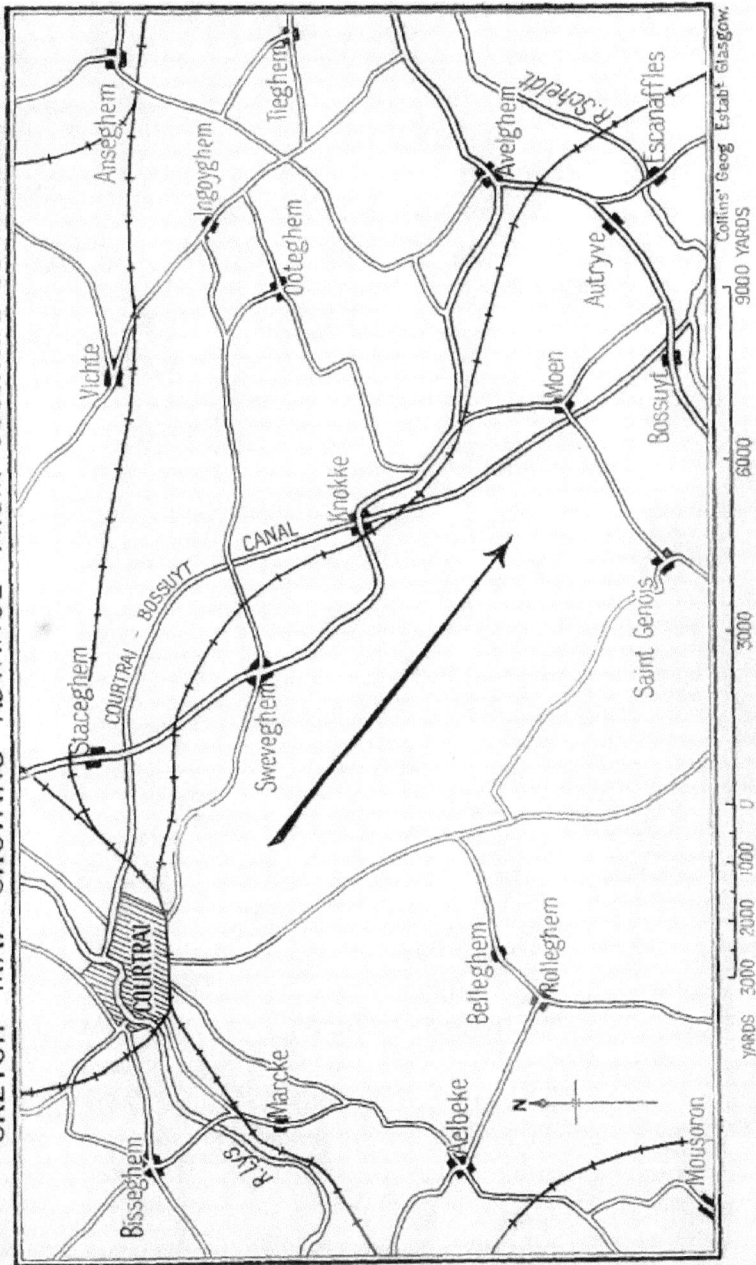

SKETCH MAP SHOWING ADVANCE FROM COURTRAI TO SCHELDT

Anseghem
Tieghem
R. Scheldt
Aveighem
Escanaffles
Ingoyghem
Ooteghem
Autryve
Vichte
Moen
Bossuyt
Knokke
CANAL
Saint Genois
Staceghem
COURTRAI - BOSSUYT
Sweveghem
COURTRAI
Belleghem
Rolleghem
Marcke
R. Lys
Aelbeke
Bisseghem
N
Mousoron

YARDS 3000 2000 1000 0 3000 6000 9000 YARDS

headquarters of two sections, Royal Engineers. Yet you wouldn't offer it to a tramp at home and a pig would scorn it—great are the blessings of civilisation!

I decided to keep one section in reserve, so took No. 3 up the line for night work.

Arrived very late as all the tracks were knee-deep in slush and it was dark, dark as the inside of an *infidel*.

We floundered around for several hours, but it was quite impossible to do anything in the nature of serious work—the line was new to us, and the difficulty of finding the posts was increased by persistent machine-gun fire and the most devilish weather imaginable. The ground was in an awful state, and it often took us twenty minutes to move a hundred yards—the men swore sublimely and their humour was the only dryness in the night.

On the return journey we struck some unpleasant shell-fire, and mud wallowed with enthusiasm. Browning anticipated the Great War when he wrote—

> *Will sprawl—*
> *Flat on his belly in the pit's much mire,*
> *With elbows wide, fists clenched to prop his chin,*
> *And, while he kicks both feet in the cool slush,*
> *And feels about his spine small eft-things course,*
> *Run in and out each arm, and make him laugh.*

Twice we got lost in the woods and finally I had to give up all hope of finding the lake track. We returned the long way, but even so the tracks were knee-deep and I could feel the water trickling in over the tops of my field boots. Sometimes it would be such a relief if only one could cry!

The men had a drop of rum when we got back, and it was about 4 a.m. when I crawled into my flea bag. A family of beetles played, "Come and sit on my chair" across my toes, and an old brown rat wanted to keep me company. I turned him out three times, but the poor devil was so persistent and so pathetic that finally I let him stop. Immediately I fell asleep he came and stroked my hair in gratitude and I, misunderstanding his intentions, turned him out for good and all.

But have you ever tried to sleep in your soaking wet clothes, with your head two feet under a sheet of corrugated iron on which it is raining hard? I tried, but the rain and the beetles were against me. I got up, and the morning and the evening were the first day.

*Sept. 10.* Still raining; and we spent another awful night in the outpost line. Our own 18-pounders were shooting so short that some of the shells were actually falling behind us and once we had to lie on the Bosche side of the parapet to get cover from them. The weather is our most dangerous foe now, and all wiring etc. is stopped until we can make some sort of protection for the line troops. They are going down like flies, there isn't a dugout worth the name in the whole sector, and the water, already a foot deep in the best posts, is increasing hourly.

*Sept. 11.* Another terrible night—it is still raining and we have been soaked through now for four days and nights. Most of the companies are down to half strength and trench-foot is very prevalent—it is as much as most of the men can do to carry two sheets of iron per night for their own protection. Our own billets are flooded now and we are knee-deep in mud everywhere—the horses feel it more than we do and I have had to send them back. We had to shift their position every three or four hours to prevent them sinking, and it has been so bitterly cold—there is no protection from this biting wind as it howls and shrieks across the swamps and mud fields.

But one thinks of the line, for it is always the line, poor devils, who get it worst—they could tell Dante many things.

There are men up there who have not been under a shelter of any description during a week of almost continuous rain—they have forgotten what it is to feel dry, and their minds are dull and stupid with the cold and misery of it all—they have slept fitfully, wakening under the necessity of shifting their position to avoid the mud or when an unusually fierce downpour has stung their faces—and during the whole of this time no warm food or drink has passed their lips. Small wonder that they die—with

ROYAL ENGINEERS AT WORK

gratitude.

*Sept. 12.* It is two feet deep on our best main road, and we had a wild fight last night to get the necessary material up for the shelters—an unlucky shell killed two men, wounded three, and knocked out two mules. In spite of this we did a good night's work and erected fourteen shelters. The men seem to realise how much depends on them, and I have seldom seen them work so well.

*Sept. 13.* Heavy shelling on roads and tracks disorganised all parties and interfered with work. I was hit in the middle of the back with a large fragment which bruised me badly.

If I stumbled and fell once last night, I fell twenty times—we use three-quarters of our strength in fighting through the mud and the remaining quarter in actual work. We were so tired last night that I tried the short way back again through the woods. Once we stumbled on a colony of rats, feeding on the sodden corpse of a Frenchman. I shuddered involuntarily as they scattered away, screaming, and then turned to watch us with beady, malevolent eyes.

The last time I was home on leave I remember my mother asked me why the trench rats were so big. I nearly told her, but then it occurred to me that I might be "missing" myself and the thought would have driven her mad—so I said it was because of the food we used to throw over the top. God help the mothers who really know these things.

Derry crocked up again yesterday and went to hospital.

*Sept. 14.* It is still raining and we are still mud-slinging— would that I had the time to describe it all.

My back was very sore today and I could hardly raise my right arm on account of the smack I received last night.

The morale of the men is very low again, but fortunately the weather prevents the Huns from doing anything but shell us.

*Sept. 15.* Signs of the weather improving at last, but mud is very plentiful and we experience great difficulty in getting about. Artillery and machine-guns were very active on both sides last night, and, as we had unusually large parties out, I had a very worrying time. At one time there were 150 men bunched together on the road for nearly an hour on account of brigade giving wrong orders. It was a great relief when we were able to move them and no damage had been done—but a mistake like that frequently costs twenty lives and no one is shot for it.

About 2 a.m. I went out in front to reconnoitre a line for wire when I came across three dead Bosche in a shell-hole. One was an enormously fat man, and as I was turning him over to cut off his shoulder numbers, he grunted fiercely like a man awakening from a heavy sleep. For a moment I was horrified and put my hand on my revolver and waited, for perhaps half a minute, undecided what to do. Then I saw the truth. The noise which had startled me was due to the gases of decomposition being forced through his mouth when I turned him over—another of the glories of war!

*Sept. 16.* A really fine day at last and out spirits rise accordingly—-our hopes are drowning and we have to clutch at the flimsiest of straws. Last night was very quiet and a lot of good work was done. The men went back about 4 a.m. and I turned into Battalion H.Q. for a pow-wow with the colonel. As I was walking home about half an hour afterwards the Hun put down a very heavy gas-shell bombardment, particularly around the track. I lay in a hole for half an hour with my mask on and was frightened to death lest I should be splashed with some of the infernal liquid. The shells were not more than 18-pounders, but some of them were unpleasantly close. This morning division reports that some 3000 shells came over in the half-hour.

A new officer joined us today. He is about thirty, wears gold-rimmed glasses, and has never seen the war before. He looks around with the wonderment of a little child and will be an infernal nuisance to us. Still, I suppose there are no real men left now.

*Sept. 17.* Spent the night by myself crawling around in front and noting the places most in need of wire. I came across a German post with four men in it and a light machine-gun. They were well forward, quite isolated and obviously nervous. I told the nearest company, but they wouldn't do anything, and even looked frightened to think that there were real live Germans so near them.

A sod splashed down in the trench outside, and I noticed the orderly at the door, a lad about eighteen, jump and nearly drop his rifle. It all makes one very sad if you look back upon the days when there would have been a clamour to go and snaffle that post. And this is the division which captured and lost one village seven times on one bloody day, and finally held it against all attacks with a fifth of its effectives on their feet.

*Sept. 18.* The men went back into reserve billets today, but I stayed on with the relieving sections. The ground is beginning to dry again and life becomes more pleasant.

There is great aerial activity and the Hun shoots very much on our roads and back areas—surely, we are not preparing a stunt?

*Sept. 19.* Received orders to return to reserve billets as we are going out of the line. Spent a busy day handing over work and packing up, as the whole company moves tomorrow.

*Sept. 20.* Trekked to our new billets in reserve, which are almost out of the war—even the 60-pounders are well in front of us. Spent a quiet day making cover for the men, rigging up horse-lines, and generally settling down. There is more billeting accommodation than we have seen for months and, greatest joy of all, we can sleep in our pyjamas.

*Sept. 21.* Apparently, there is some kind of a stunt coming off, because we have instructions to rest the men as much as possible and give them an easy time. Accordingly, we do a little drill, paint our transport, clean rifles and ammunition, overhaul explosives, etc., etc.

There is some fascination about this war game, some inexplicable grip which it has over us. In spite of everything we have gone through there is, once more, a thrill of expectation in the air, and the men seem keener, as though looking forward to

BENDING RAIL

LAYING RAILS

something.

No one could hate war more than I do, and yet I would be bitterly disappointed if sent on leave tomorrow. And if we, of all men, can still feel moments of exhilaration, can there ever be a League of Nations?

*Sept. 22.* The usual instruction work and overhauling of equipment. Orders came through today that we are to give the men instruction in attack, open warfare, and extended order formations. The men enjoy it and are cheering up tremendously. There are now several new divisions in our area, guns are coming forward and more troops arrive every day, all of them apparently from the south. They seem fresher and more confident than out own men, but they have already had the experience of driving Huns before them—we, on the other hand, have been fighting a losing fight with our backs to the wall for over seven months. A lot of kilted troops arrived today.

*Sept. 23.* Had the men out all day practising attack formations. It is hard to believe that these fiercely rushing groups of men are the same troops who were fought to a standstill at Kemmel, and held that blood-soaked line with such dogged fatalism through the weary summer. And after two or three days' rest they are expected to go forward again—a man must feel proud!

*Sept. 24.* Training hard. In spite of high hopes dashed before, we seem as keen as ever to make another effort. The atmosphere seems charged with electricity, more troops are pouring in, and the broad-gauge railway is up nearly as far as our billets. Was recommended again for an M.C.—this time due to appear in the King's Christmas Honours List.

*Sept. 25.* We are still without orders, but the attack must be near at hand now—expectation and excitement.

*Sept. 26.* Received preliminary orders that Day and I will take a section each and join the artillery brigades to make roads and bridges for them in the advance. Two sections remain in reserve under Cooper. Attack before dawn on the 28th.

Went up to the brigade to arrange details and went to bed on return. Roused after an hour's sleep to go out with a section to repair two forward bridges near the front line before daybreak.

Got about twenty men and miscellaneous material on to two pontoon wagons and started out in drizzling rain. I sat in the front of the first wagon, and as we lumbered off into the dark, I fell into a sort of reverie. I thought lazily of home and of the 28th, and the things it might mean, and in my mind I went again over the characters of the men, the good ones and the doubtful ones, and detailed them off for different jobs— these and a thousand other thoughts wandered idly through my mind, punctuated by the jolting of the wagon and the barking of the 18-pounders. Then the men began to sing, very quietly and sweetly, and the rise and fall of their voices seemed to add some special significance to the night. We made good progress over the bad roads, stopping occasionally to check our way or adjust a girth.

Now they were singing "Annie Laurie," and I heard Garner say "Damn" under his breath. I asked him what was the matter with them tonight, and he said, "Dunno, sir, but I wish they wouldn't sing like that." The rain had developed into a heavy Scotch mist which swallowed up the lead driver and the mounted corporal. I shivered under my coat, and felt unutterably lonely and sad.

At last the wagons stopped and we went forward on foot towards the work. We bridged three trenches and then came to the main job, a 15-foot span across a swollen *beek*, and not more than 400 yards from the German lines. For about an hour the work went quietly and well and we got an arch across the stream in the form of an old French steel shelter.

Suddenly there was a short, fierce whine, a crash, and a livid burst of flame right in the party—three more followed almost instantaneously and then for a second an awful silence. Someone said "Christ!" and began to cry gently. Five men were killed, three of them practically missing, and three badly wounded. By a miracle the work was practically undamaged.

We took the casualties to the wagons and returned to the job—how the men worked there again I shall never know, but

Engineers repairing a bridge

Royal Engineers bridging a stream

they did, and the bridge was across an hour before dawn. The suddenness of the shock has knocked my nerves to pieces and even as I write my hand trembles.

Looking back now I can see something unnatural in the whole of that ride in the pontoons—little details were too impressive, and there was an almost unhuman beauty in the way they sang that song. I am sure that some of those men had a vague premonition of what was coming.

*Sept. 27.* Lay down for a few hours after we got back, but was unable to sleep. At midday I took Nos. 2 and 3 Sections to forward billets at Pig-stye Farm, and at 5 p.m. No. 3 Section moved out again to join their brigade. The company transport and reserve sections arrived about 9 p.m.

Major and I had a final talk together, and I turned in about 11 p.m. I was nervous and excited, and although very tired, slept but little.

*Sept. 28.* No. 2 Section breakfasted at 2.15 a.m. and were ready on the road at 3.30. Whilst I was inspecting them the barrage started on our left for the Belgian attack, and the northern sky was bubbling with light.

We reached Brigade H.Q. at the *château* about 5.15 and at 5.30 our barrage started and the front line troops went over. The scheme was that we were to go forward at once and make a track passable for 18-pounders from their present positions up to second jumping-off line. They were expected to be there about noon and would then be in a position to support the further advance of the infantry. Everything depended on getting the field guns forward to support the second attack.

I left the transport at the *château* under the corporal and led the men forward towards a half-dried-up canal which was the first break in the road. It was raining heavily.

It soon became apparent that the Germans were maintaining a barrage on this side of the canal, and as time was against us, we had got to go through it. It looked rough and ugly and the men were looking at each other. For a moment I was tempted—we were absolutely alone and it was up to me—nobody could blame us if we didn't go through, and in an hour it would probably have stopped.

We were perhaps five hundred yards from the canal and shells were bursting heavily—there was no cover and at times the canal banks were obscured by the fumes and smoke from the bursts. Something outside a man takes hold of him at these times and tells him what to do. In half a minute I was calmly saying, "Come on," and the men were following in single file, about ten paces from man to man.

I thought we should never get across—we tried to run but we kept sticking in the mud and bunching together—just like a nightmare. Once or twice I looked round and the men were grand—two fellows were hit and the others dragged them across—then a third went down and was picked up by the two behind—eventually we were under the shelter of the canal bank with one man killed and two wounded. It was great, and after that I felt we could do anything.

By now we were soaked to the skin, but bunches of prisoners were coming back and the worst seemed to be over. We worked steadily on the roads under fairly continuous shell-fire, and by 10 a.m. the track was completed. After this the German shell-fire weakened as the advance went forward and his guns were either taken or forced to withdraw. The men were worn out and literally covered with mud, so I withdrew to some old dug-outs in the canal bank. A message was sent for the transport to come forward and another one to the company for rum.

The men had just lit fires and were beginning to dry themselves when I received a message that the guns had reached their destination but our further help was wanted at once. At 11.30 the section moved forward again, and by 2 p.m. the whole brigade were standing to for action in their new positions. The division moved up into line during the afternoon and the advance pushed Wytschaete-Messines, and the Warneton line are reported captured.

At 4 p.m. the section returned to the canal, awaiting further orders. The brigade commander personally thanked me for the day's work. At 4.30 I received news that the transport was stuck somewhere behind us, but they were trying to get the limber forward with six horses in it instead of the normal two—the tool-cart had been abandoned. Eventually the limber arrived and then I sent four horses back for the tool-cart which arrived about 6.30 *via* Ypres—the roads are in a terrible state and will do more than the Huns to hold us up.

At 7.0 the men had a meal—the first since 2 a.m. this morning—and after that turned in to a more than well-earned rest. I went over to see the colonel and learnt that they are pushing on over the hills and Comines is to be captured tomorrow. Everyone is delighted, the show has been a great success and casualties are light in comparison with the results—the only trouble is the mud, with which we are literally covered from head to foot.

*Sept. 29.* Our rations arrived about 5 a.m., but no forage for the horses, and we were unable to move forward in consequence—my biggest trouble is going to be to keep in touch with supplies and water during this nomadic life. Roads were reported passable as far as the front, so I left the section standing to under the sergeant and rode off to find the company. I hunted about all morning and found them at last at the old place but just ready to move off. Arranged to draw rations direct from the company each day with my own limber.

I took two nose-bags of corn back with me on my mare, gave the limber horses a feed when I reached the section, and then sent them back for rations. Somehow or other the company has heard some very highly-coloured accounts of our passage through the barrage on the 28th.

At 2 p.m. I rode forward with an orderly and visited the brigade and all batteries. Heavy rain set in again, and as everyone seemed fairly comfortable and there was no accommodation forward, I decided to spend another night at the canal. The road is blocked with traffic from morning till night, and I am afraid it will break up badly if the rain continues—the whole show depends on that one, blessed road, and apparently it is going to be my job for two or three days more until the corps troops can get up.

The brigade was in action when I reached them and a stiff

British troops at the site of Ypres town in British West Flanders, Sept. 29th, 1918

fight was going on around the last ridges—the Huns are sticking a bit and a fierce counter-attack had just been driven back—rifle and machine-gun fire was very intense. I saw a lot of Hun dead about the roads and a few of our fellows. The Huns have left a lot of guns behind and should be fairly hard hit.

It was dark when I got back, and the horses could hardly crawl along. Rations and forage came up shortly afterwards, so we turned in and had a good night's rest.

*Sept. 30.* Heavy rain all last night. At 8 a.m. I sent two orderlies up to brigade and my groom back to the company to change my mare—she was completely exhausted. Pending receipt of orders, we rigged up a shelter for the horses, as they were shivering badly and I began to be frightened for them—the poor beasts are caked with mud, and even their eyes are hardly free from it.

At noon received orders to go forward as early as possible, so I sent half the limber back for rations and moved up with the section. After a really terrific struggle we got as far as the batteries and managed to find a bit of cover in some old German concrete dug-outs. Worked till dark on the road and then started to fix things up for the night. The dug-outs were in the middle of a swamp about 500 yards from the road, and in the dark it took us threequarters of an hour to reach them.

I had to give up all idea of getting the horses across, and finally found a place where they could stand about a mile from the dug-outs. The drivers were quite worn out, so we had to mount a stable-guard of sappers, with instructions to move the horses every hour to prevent them sinking in the mud.

It is still raining, bitterly cold, and I can't understand how the poor beasts live. The wagons are nearly axle deep. Shortly after midnight I had everyone settled and then crawled, literally, into my own shack. It is an old Bosche concrete place and stinks like Hell—there are two wooden bunks in it, but it is dry. My man lit a fire on the floor and we warmed up some old tea in my shaving mug. I was chilled to the bone and there was nothing to eat, but I shall always believe that that tea saved my life. There was no room for officer and servant there—just two very weary men, we sat on either side the fire drying our socks and the

80

smell mingled with the fetid odours of the dug-out.

Our eyes grew red and tearful with the smoke, which eventually drove us to the uninviting boards, where we slept like the Babes in the Wood. Several times during the night I woke up shivering with cold and the clammy clothes sticking to my skin, but—we were over the hills and I would not have missed that night for all the gold in Africa.

*Oct. 1.* Up at 5.30 and immensely cheered to see a blue sky, although I didn't begin to feel normally warm until about noon. Bully and biscuit for breakfast as a change from the biscuit and bully of the preceding days. Received an official note of thanks from the brigade for our work, and orders from the C.R.E. to rejoin the company. Apparently, the advance is held up for a few days until heavy guns and supplies can get forward again. I sent No. 2 Section forward to work on the new plank avoiding road and returned to meet the major at 8 a.m. He returned to the company and sent up Nos. 1 and 4 Sections to me from reserve billets. No. 3 Section also rejoined, so I fixed the lot in billets as well as possible and then took out Nos. 1, 3, 4 to work on the road with No. 2.

We have now got all out limbers and tool-carts as far as the batteries, and I am commanding all the sections—Cooper remains with the heavy transport on the other side of the mud. Rode round the work during the afternoon and met the C.R.E., who was full of congratulations. Withdrew to billets at 5 p.m. to give the men a chance to dry their clothes and have a warm meal—the first they have had since the 27th.

We are without definite news, but apparently the whole show has been a great success, and the army is only waiting until we can get the roads through. I can never forget the great change which seemed to spread like wildfire over the spirit of the army on the evening of the 28th-29th.

We were in the midst of the worst of the mud area, miles of transport wagons were bogged along out single road, it was raining hard, and few of us had eaten anything for twenty-four hours. Nobody was looking forward to the dawn. But from somewhere behind us a rumour came through that Bulgaria had asked for Peace. There was no cheering, no demonstration of any sort, but the news seemed to put new spirit into the tired troops. The weary mud-caked horses were lashed and spurred again, men put their aching shoulders to the wheels, and once more the limbers lumbered forward.

All night long the wagons toiled painfully up those fateful ridges where scores of thousands of our finest infantry had died, and in the drizzling dawn they saw their reward at last—behind them lay the dull, dead plain, with its memories of misery and mud—before them, they looked down upon a new, unbroken country, and the spire of Tenbrielen church, untouched of shot or shell, beckoned like a winning post against the eastern sky.

*Oct. 2.* Heavy rain again last night, but it hasn't damped our spirits. We could meet almost any call again now.

At 5.30 a.m. an orderly came in with orders from the C.R.E. saying that we are to work from six to nine on the divisional main road. By dashing off without any breakfast we were able to start at 7.30, and returned for a meal at noon—our first since yesterday evening. In the afternoon Day worked the sections on the road while the major and I brought up the heavy transport.

Artillery horse-lines just forward of our own were heavily shelled for about five minutes and a lot of horses were knocked out—about 100 of the poor beasts stampeded, and it was a pitiful sight to see some of them dragging their entrails along the ground. This incident made me realise that if the Germans have any fight left in them at all we are in a very precarious position. Several divisions are herded together with the River Lys in front of them and an impassable belt of swamp and mud behind. A really energetic counter-attack would give us another Cambrai.

At night many fires were visible again where the enemy is burning villages along his retreat—many of these appear to be very far off, which looks as if they contemplate a big withdrawal—a favourite theory is that they will withdraw as far as the Meuse for the winter.

*Oct. 3.* Company commenced work on a new plank road to relieve the strain on the main road.

I went forward with three wagons to a dump on the Menin

road to get material, but it took us all morning to get there as the roads were blocked with artillery limbers—we want ten times more transport and ten times more labour than we have got if we are to make any reasonable progress. The Field Companies are quite inadequate to cope with any serious road-making in an advance like this. In the afternoon scouted round with Cooper looking for what had once been a first-class road, clearly marked on our maps.

We couldn't find a stone, a tree, or any single thing that would indicate where the road had been—we couldn't even fix it from our maps, as farms, houses, and landmarks of any description had totally disappeared. We had some difficulty in getting back, and once Cooper's horse went down to her belly in the mud—we nearly lost her, but got her out eventually.

*Oct. 4.* Took all wagons to the dump and got a lot of material up during the day—made some appreciable progress on the road. Two new officers have joined us, and Day has gone back to H.Q. wagon lines. Was delighted to meet two old friends, Lucas and Mitchell of our left division, in the afternoon.

*Oct. 5.* Road is now going forward well, and we had another fine day although very cold. Things seem to be sorting themselves out after the last advance and we should soon be ready to try again.

*Oct. 6.* Orders from the C.R.E. that we shall probably move again tomorrow and all ranks are to have as much rest as possible. Worked all morning on the road and packed pontoons, etc., during the afternoon.

*Oct. 7.* Two sections moved at 7 a.m. to work again on the avoiding road, and two sections moved across country towards the Menin road. At 9 a.m. I took the transport across in front of Ypres and picked up Cooper with the pontoons in the afternoon. We made a horse-lines there, as it was the only patch of dry earth available, but before getting in we had to shift about fifteen dead mules which had been killed the night belote by a bomb.

Billeted the sections in an area containing one dug-out, just off the Ypres-Menin road—a piece of ground probably more fiercely fought over than any other during the war. The solitary dug-out was unusable owing to prevalence of dead Bosche—as Mark Twain would say, "*Fixed, so that they could outvote us.*"

We couldn't find a level piece of ground large enough to take one tent without a lot of digging. The sergeants found a very good place for their tent, but a dead Hun was in possession of the freehold. They decided to bury him, and deepened a shell-hole accordingly; then the problem, how to get him into it? The sergeant-major took his boots and the farrier very gingerly took his sleeves; they lifted, but his arms came out in the farrier's hands. They withdrew to windward and talked; it was growing dusk, the tent must go up. Finally, the farrier put his gas mask on and literally buried him in shovelfuls. *Pro patria*—

The only way to stop war is to tell these facts in the school history books and cut out the rot about the gallant charges, the victorious returns, and the blushing damsels who scatter roses under the conquering heroes' feet. Every soldier knows that a rewriting of the history books would stop war more effectively than the most elaborately covenanted league which tired politico-legal minds can conceive.

*Oct. 8.* Working all day on the roads. It is a dreary job in this blighted, featureless country.

*Oct. 9.* Received orders to report again at Artillery Brigade H.Q., so there is obviously another stunt in the wind. In the meantime, we are still mud-slinging.

*Oct. 10.* Went forward into the outposts to reconnoitre tracks and ways forward for the guns. We were in absolutely virgin country, and it was a new experience to think of death lurking behind these green hedges and quiet farm buildings. At night took the section up and did a lot of work—filled in several ditches, cleared a ride through a wood, and chopped down several trees with which we made a small bridge—took the floor out of the farm kitchen to cover it with.

*Oct. 11.* Out reconnoitring again all morning, and at night took a company of pioneers up to work on a second track. Had a very unpleasant time on the Menin road, where we were heavily shelled—some artillery transport suffered badly, but we got through without casualties.

The weather continues fine, and everything points to another show about the 15th. The Huns have put up a lot of wire, but the field guns have been shooting this down steadily for three days now, and the heavies are coming into position. This morning when I was up, our shells were falling dead in the belts of wire and cutting broad lanes through it. Sent in two recommendations for Military Medals for work in the last show:—

MOUNTED CORPORAL.—For great gallantry and devotion to duty in bringing up transport and supplies under heavy shell-fire and at great personal risk. His action greatly contributed to the success of the section in its work of helping forward the guns.

A SAPPER.—For conspicuous gallantry and devotion to duty when repairing a bridge under heavy shell-fire for the advance of the artillery. He set a fine example to his comrades, and persevered with his work until it was completed, regardless of great personal danger.

It was hard to write the above, knowing that every man equally deserves those medals—the whole institution of awards ought to be abolished; except, perhaps, the V.C.

*Oct. 12.* Skipper returned from leave. Company still carrying on with roads. No. 2 Section out with me all night widening a bridge. It was a miserable night with heavy rain and howling wind, but the men worked cheerfully and a lot of work was done. So far as we are concerned all is now ready for the next attack.

*Oct. 13.* The attack is to start early on the morning of the 14th, and will be general along the army front. The company received orders to more forward today, but I had to go on to brigade before they started or before I knew exactly where they were going. I left brigade shortly after dusk and returned to find two companies of pioneers who were detailed to work under me tomorrow. I knew they were somewhere in the morass near the Menin road, but I blundered about for two hours before I found them.

It required all my will power to keep me going, and when finally I saw their tents I was in the last stages of exhaustion—several times I must have been very near to them, but it was impossible to see more than 20 yards, and I had passed away again, going round and round in circles. I was so weak towards the end that I used to lie still in the mud for several minutes every time I fell, aching in every muscle, and wondering how many more times I could fall without dropping off to sleep.

It was after 1 a.m. when I left the pioneers and there was a four-mile walk to where I thought the company would be. I wandered from battery to battery asking for news of them, but no one could tell me where they were. It was absolutely vital that I should find them before dawn, but at last my legs failed completely and I collapsed in the middle of the road. I crawled into a hole in the bank but, tired as I was, couldn't sleep because of the cold. I was tormented with fears as to what would happen in the morning as I was the only officer who knew the gun tracks and almost everything depended on the clearing of those.

*Oct. 14.* Dawn came at last, cold, clear, and very beautiful, and at 5.35 the barrage came to spoil it. I set off towards the batteries in the hope of picking the men up there and found the Pioneers. I gave them work to go on with and turned to try to find my own fellows. The din from our own guns was terrific and the German retaliation seemed unusually heavy. The hard, persistent rattle of machine-gun fire in front seemed to indicate that we had stuck and a lot of wounded seemed to be coming back—some shells exploded very near me and I dropped into a ditch. I was cold, hungry, and tired, and at that moment would have sold my soul to have been out of it all. Above me the sky was serenely blue and peaceful, but eastwards it was shot with balls of multi-coloured smoke, just as if an invisible artist were dabbing splotches of colour on to a blue canvas.

Why, oh! why should I walk into that blazing inferno and die on a morning like this? These thoughts were actually in my mind when I saw Cooper coming down the road with the section—they thought I had been killed. I shall always remember standing there in the road and chewing ravenously at a hunk of bully which I held in my muddy fingers. It was my first meal for seventeen hours, and I never enjoyed one better.

Then we went forward, and I began to get hold of myself again as the work engaged my attention. I shall never forget one sight. A big highlander with the lower part of his face blown off walking down the railway with a prisoner in front of him—his right hand on the back of the German's neck and his left hand holding his face together with the blood pouring through his fingers. Men coming back say the Huns stuck hard at first, but we are going well forward now.

Today's programme was roughly as follow:—

The Army Corps is to form bridgeheads across the River Lys for a defensive flank. One R.E. company takes all the divisional pontoons and stands by to bridge when the infantry get to the river. One section of this to dash forward with Lewis guns and try to prevent destruction of existing bridges. The second company and two of our own sections are working on roads with special instructions to search for and destroy land mines. One of our remaining sections reporting on German dumps, and generally gathering information, and the last section arranging temporary water supplies.

We went forward very well during the morning as there was practically no shell-fire after the first two hours. The losses seem to have been fairly heavy in forcing the first trenches, and there were a lot of bodies lying crumpled up among the German wire. All that we saw were the veriest youngsters, and they looked so out of place lying there dead in the green fields on this beautiful autumn morning. Shortly after noon we arrived at a large farm and found ourselves mixed up with the front line infantry, who were held up. We lay behind a hedge and got a few shots into a feeble German counter-attack, and after this the line went forward again.

NEAR THE RIVER LYS

We remained at the farm and about two o'clock were heavily shelled by German field guns. Several machine-gunners were hit and the brigade commander, who had just arrived, had his leg blown off. For a few minutes the place was in chaos, but two 18-pounders galloped up and silenced the Hun battery with their first few shots. After these years of trench warfare, it is wonderful to see field guns galloping into action and engaging the enemy over open sights.

Beyond the farm the roads were in perfect condition, so we returned to the company and found them in tents on a hill about three miles behind. I thought at one time the men would have to carry me back, I had never felt so tired. Bad news awaited us—Cooper had been killed early in the morning, about half an hour after the attack started—later in the day the sergeant-major was wounded, and there were eleven casualties among the men.

The passing of an old friend makes a big impression in a small mess, and we were very silent at night as we sat and smoked after supper. The town of Menin was burning fiercely and many other places farther to the east.

*Oct. 15.* Buried Cooper fairly decently in some old sacking at a Belgian cemetery. No orders came through, and we had a day of welcome rest.

*Oct. 16.* Company moved forward at 10.30 a.m. to battle areas and took over billets from a company of our left division. There are no signs of war here, and almost every man in the company has a bed to sleep in—splendid grazing for the horses and lots of vegetables in the fields for ourselves. It is all like fairyland, and we walked out solemnly this afternoon to look at a large green field without a single shell-hole in it.

Reports state that we have taken Courtrai, and streams of refugees coming back along the roads indicate that it may be true. Unfortunately, they are all of the very lowest classes, and as they only speak Flemish, we were unable, to get any information out of them. It is a heart-breaking sight to see them trudging through the rain—old men, women, and the tiniest of children. Sometimes they wheel a barrow containing a few of their goods, but most of them are without anything except the miserable rags they stand in.

*Oct. 17.* Had the company out all day doing road drainage. The tedium of the work was relieved by a ghastly incident, showing how low these poor refugees have sunk. A party of them were trudging listlessly along the road when the leaders noticed a dead horse lying in the ditch. In a few seconds the men and women had taken their knives and were fighting like animals on the distended carcass, chattering and shrieking like a crowd of hungry jackals. As they worked, they threw the chunks of bleeding meat into the road, where the children fought for them and stowed them in the barrows. In a few minutes the horse was stripped to his bones, the noise subsided, and the ghouls trudged on their way.

*Oct. 18.* Working on the road all day in heavy rain, but were called out again at night to form a bridgehead across the river in front of us. We are in possession of half the town on the near side of the river, but the Germans have destroyed all the bridges and hold the eastern half of the town. The main road bridge in the centre of the town lay across the bed of the river in a maze of twisted steel-work—we were required to make a foot bridge across these ruins for the infantry to get across. Day climbed across with three men and a Lewis gun on the ruins of the old bridge and cleared a German machine-gun party out of the farther bank.

After this we started work and made fair progress considering the vile conditions. With the river sucking and swirling below them and the cold rain numbing their fingers, it was anything but an easy task for the men to keep their foothold on the slippery, twisted girders. In addition, we were shelled persistently through the night, and seven men were down when the first infantry went across about 4.0 a.m.

*Oct. 19.* An hour after our return to billets orders came through for us to move forward again. The other companies got two pontoon bridges across the river during the day and we billeted near at hand, to provide maintenance parties. I was very tired and turned into bed early, looking forward to a long night's sleep.

Just as I was dozing off the orderly corporal came in with a message from the bridge patrol asking me to go out as numerous things were going wrong. There is no worse torture for a really tired man than to allow him to get into a warm, comfortable bed for a few minutes and then turn him out into a stormy night. And I had been living all day on the strength of the night's sleep that I was going to get!

Arrived at the bridges I had no time for regrets—the river was rising, the traffic was absolutely continuous, and everything that could go wrong was doing so.

However, we kept them going all night long with the exception of a twenty-minute stopping of one bridge, and Day relieved me at 6 a.m. I was relieved in more senses than one, for two or three times during the night I felt things getting too much for me, things that I would have enjoyed three years ago. Wild, angry thoughts went running through my mind as we struggled with that creaking, groaning bridge, and nursed it through the weary hours—and worst of all, the bitter thought that so long as we succeeded none of the sleeping millions at home would ever hear of the work we did. And thousands of men all over France were doing just the same

*That the Sons of Mary may overcome it,*
*Pleasantly sleeping and unaware.*

Why should I be alone there in the dark with that nerve-racking responsibility, and why should we splash in that freezing water, heaving anchors, tightening trestle chains, and baling the leaky pontoons?—and all unknown!

These are bitter thoughts, but I am worn out for months I have been living on my will power, but my body and my nerves were exhausted a year ago. I find it cynically amusing to wonder what the idealistic, rugby-playing self of 1913 would think of this introspective, nerve-shattered crock. He would have sniffed and turned away—as the world will do when we return.

*Oct. 20.* Standing to all day under one hour's notice to move as the forward division are attacking the ridge which overlooks the Scheldt. In the evening we heard that the attack was held up and failed, and we are to try our luck tomorrow. At 9.30 p.m. I rode forward with No. 2 Section with orders to join the fusiliers before dawn. It was abnormally dark, raining persistently, and I had the greatest difficulty in finding our way—worst of all, I had to conquer an ever-growing feeling that I didn't care whether I found it or not—even that little responsibility was too much for me. I wanted to be alone to cry. After two hours I fell into a coma and then dismounted and walked to prevent myself giving way altogether.

We found the brigade at 3 a.m., and I put the men into a barn for two hours' rest. I gave orders to be called at five, and turned into an armchair in the farmhouse kitchen.

For the first time since I came to France my nerves gave way completely and I was tormented with fears of the morrow. I had just been told that we were to go forward with the fusiliers against the banks of a canal and help them across as well as we could—there would be machine-gun fire and no cover. Those were the facts. We have done infinitely worse a thousand times and thought nothing of it.

But I lay in that chair for two hours actually shivering with fear and apprehension. My crazy mind wouldn't rest, and I saw myself killed in a dozen different ways as we rushed for the canal bank—at one time I had the wildest impulse to run away and hide until the attack was over. I knew that was impossible, and then I thought I would report sick and pretend to faint. I was ready to do anything except face machine-gun fire again—once we got so close that I could see a German's face leering behind his gun and the familiar death rattle was as loud as thunder in my ears. I sat and watched my hand shaking on the edge of the chair and had no more control over it than if it had belonged to someone else.

Somehow, I pulled together when the orderly corporal came, paraded the section, mechanically inspected the tools, and then marched off. In ten minutes, I was myself again and at 6.30 we reached the fusiliers. At 7.0 the advance commenced in drizzling rain and we moved forward over the sodden fields.

*Oct. 21.* It was very misty at first, and the whole affair reminded me of a Laffan's Plain manoeuvre—the scattered groups of men worked steadily forward over the open fields and occasionally a nervous civilian would take a peep at us from a farmhouse window—there was no sign of war except, perhaps, an unnatural stillness which seemed to hang over the countryside like a mist. It gave one an uncanny feeling, this blundering forward in the mist across an unknown country—the only certainty, that Death was in front and that we must walk on until He declared Himself.

By eleven we were within a thousand yards of the canal and could dimly see the general line of the banks in front of us. Here, at least, we knew that there would be resistance, but as yet there came no sound from the rising ground in front. The ground between us and the canal was very open, so we rested some minutes behind the last thick hedges and took the opportunity of reorganising the units. Then we went forward again, a long straggling line of crouching figures who cursed and panted as they toiled over the swampy ground.

At last the storm broke, heavy machine-gun fire but at rather long range. The line flopped down into the mud, and groups of men began to work forward in short rushes to a ditch in front which seemed to offer cover. We reached this with very few casualties, but the fire was too hot for further progress. Sniping continued all day, and in places we pushed two or three hundred yards nearer to the canal. No. 2 Section took refuge in a farmhouse and awaited developments.

After dusk I crawled forward with Jennings of the fusiliers and got through on to the canal towpath—there were a lot of Huns round the canal and their outposts were fully 300 yards on our side of it. After some difficulty we got within about 50 yards of the bridge and I noticed that the Huns could still crawl across, although it was badly damaged—allowing for further demolitions I didn't think we should have much trouble in getting a footbridge across the ruins—we were nearly caught once, and lay between the water and the towpath while a party of about ten Huns walked along the path not ten feet away. Got back safely in the small hours and had a short rest in soaking clothes on the farmhouse floor.

I am too exhausted to feel tired.

*Oct. 22.* Apparently, some of our people have got across the canal farther to the north, and at 9 a.m. the attack was resumed on that side with a view to forcing the Huns out of their position. Our orders were to co-operate by means of a demonstration against the canal, but the machine-gun fire was too heavy and we could do nothing except waste a lot of ammunition. I only remember seeing a German once during the whole day, and yet the slightest exposure on our part was answered by an immediate burst of fire—they stuck it very well, because the fighting on their right flank was very heavy and they would all have been taken if we had got through.

For several hours during the morning the rifle and machine-gun fire on our left was very heavy, and the 18-pounders were continuously in action. Towards noon a battery of 68-pounders came into action and also some howitzers—several fires broke out in the houses, but the shells had no effect on the concealed gunners in the canal banks, and we waited in vain for the blue rocket that was to signal us forward. About two o'clock an intelligence officer came round and we learnt that the Germans stuck very hard this morning—we made practically no progress as a result of the battle, and our losses have been heavy.

At 4.30 the attack on our left was resumed, and the Queens made a very gallant advance which brought them down almost as far as our left flank on the canal—unfortunately, there was no support, and before dusk the weary men had to retreat to their original positions.

On our immediate right there was very little opposition, and the Durhams are firmly established across the canal. Farther south, however, our right division repeated the performance of the Queens on a larger scale and had to abandon a hardly-won bridgehead across the river after a day of strenuous fighting.

At 8 p.m. I was informed by brigade that owing to the retirement of the Queens I was covering a half-mile gap, and "should take steps accordingly." I mounted a piquet with the Lewis gun a few hundred yards forward of the farm, and sent out patrols every half-hour, but the night passed off without incident. I took out two patrols myself but could find neither our own people nor Huns.

We have had a bad day today—hard fighting, heavy losses, and no progress—people at home seem to think that we are chasing a beaten army which runs so fast that we cannot keep in touch with them. Would that it were true; but we have been badly mauled today and there is precious little offensive spirit in our nineteen-year-olds. I saw a boy of the Middlesex coming back with a finger shot away—they had run against a farmhouse with three Huns and a machine-gun and had lost four men in taking it. He said that the bloody "die hards" had lived up to their name again—four casualties!

And yet there was a day on Zandvoorde Ridge when twenty-three men, left out of 800, lay behind the piled-up bodies of their dead and held the line against the flower of the Pomeranian Guard—and they didn't talk of "die hards."

*Oct. 23.* The brigade was taken out of the line this morning and at noon we had rejoined our transport. We were under orders to move almost at once and dragged ourselves wearily on to the road, the men singing a doleful dirge, "I'm sure we can't stick it no longer." For the sake of example, I hobbled too, but would have sold my soul to get on Rosie's back—to kill the temptation I loaded four men's packs across her.

After dark we came across a battery of field guns standing-to with their trails half across the road—by skilful driving and occasionally taking a wheel over the trails we got the limbers and the tool-carts past, but it was too much for the last pontoon—her off hind-wheel hit a trail, the wheel horses slipped on the *pavé*, and the whole contraption slithered sideways into the ditch. I wanted to cry, but fortunately found the necessary relief in telling the gunners what I thought of them. It took us almost an hour to get the wagon clear, and it was midnight belote the men were into billets. There was a pile of straw for me in front of a roaring fire in the farmhouse kitchen. I collapsed on to this, too exhausted even to loosen my boots or my tunic collar.

*Oct. 24.* Let there be no mistake—last night was the happiest night of my life, and getting up at six o'clock this morning was the most wonderful thing that I have ever done. I looked into a mirror and realised with amusement why the old farmer was so terrified when I staggered in last night. The scar under my left eye is still prominent, my clothes were sodden and even my tousled hair was matted with mud; with the exception of my tunic all my uniform is standard Tommy outfit, and I wore a five-days' growth of beard—surely a more unkempt looking brigand never masqueraded as a British officer.

I looked at my great murderous maulers and wondered idly how they had evolved from the sensitive, manicured fingers that used to pen theses on *Colloidal Fuel* and *The Theory of Heat Distribution in Cylinder Walls.* And I found the comparison good.

No orders came through for us during the day, but we heard that another early morning attack on the canal had failed—all honour to those Hun machine-gunners.

After a day of strenuous cleaning, the company paraded in the afternoon and looked ready once more for anything that Hell could offer. I counted the faces that I could remember from the beginning, but there were very few left—and myself the only officer. It struck me, too, that the very men left were the ones who had run the greatest risks—hard-bitten devils like Stephens, who had been in the thick of every mess the company had struck—perhaps it is true that where there is no fear there is no danger.

*Oct. 25.* Spent another quiet day, but was rushed into the war again at very short notice in the evening. Out all night with two sections assisting forward company to put a trestle bridge across the canal lower down. There was an enormous German timber dump close at hand, and although most of the yard was burning fiercely, we saved enough material to make an excellent job of the bridge. The German engineers are very thorough in their demolitions, and have made a perfect ruin of miles of this canal—apparently their explosive charges are much more liberal than we use ourselves.

Returned to the company in a drizzling dawn, but were cheered to note droves of prisoners along the road and hear that we have gone forward again.

*Oct. 26.* At 4.30 received orders to move company to billets in a farm far behind us and near to Courtrai—-obviously to undergo a fattening process for further slaughter. After our arrival in the evening I had another of my black fits for no reason whatever—they occur more frequently now, and I must surely break up soon. The sober truth is that I am about as much use here now as my grandmother would be. But even if I am a wreck it is sweet to feel that I have wanted ten times more smashing than any of the others—I have given the Fates a run for their money and I believe I blew them once or twice.

*Oct. 27.* I have been in the saddle all day and feel like a king tonight. Silence and peace over the whole quiet countryside, and, as I rode home in the twilight, a touch of frost in the air to catch the horse's breath and make my blood tingle. Oh! It was good to be alive, to feel the power of the horse beneath me, to feel the strength returning to my own shattered body and, above all, to think of cheerful firesides down there among the trees, where the wood smoke mingled with the gathering mists. It was—

> *that sweet mood,*
> *When pleasant thoughts*
> *Bring sad thoughts to the mind.*

I saw an English village with a quaint old Norman church, and there, too, the mists were gathering in the meadows round about.

*Oct. 28.* Now we know why we are here—to train, practise, and rehearse for the crossing of the Scheldt. all the Corps Engineers met in conference in the town and spent the day designing and testing various types of footbridge. The men had the pontoons out and the officers spent the day in polishing up their drill. I saw where we crossed the first time in the driving rain, with the machine-guns hammering in the houses in front of us, and I saw the spot where I nursed the first pontoon bridge through an interminable night. But how different now!

A company of Canadian Railway troops were making a permanent bridge on the very spot where my crazy pontoons had all but foundered. A broad-gauge loco was hauling ballast up to the very edge of the river, and a steam pile-driver hissed and chattered over the trestles.

After all, our pontoons had played their part and it was comforting to see how our feeble, vanguard efforts were followed up.

Returned to the farm, I was delighted to hear that the recommendations for Military Medals had passed through—my own D.S.O. has dwindled into another "mention in despatches." *Oct. 29.* More conferences and bridgebuilding. I have been asked to reconnoitre the existing bridges over the river, and the Huns are half a mile on this side of them! Spent several hours studying maps and aeroplane photos and discussing ways and means.

*Oct. 30.* More conferences and training. Completed my plans and decided to take Stephens out with me on the night of the 31st.

*Oct. 31.* At 2.30 p.m. I lay down quite peacefully, intending to sleep until dusk, when I could set out on my venture. I was looking forward to it, and felt perfectly confident. Just as I was dozing off the orderly corporal came in, bringing, of all things, a warrant for me to go on leave tomorrow. Instantly the whole affair changed, and I was seized with a blue shivering funk. In six hours, I was due to go through the German lines, and there, lying on the table was a bit of paper waiting to take me to England in the morning. It was the cruellest stroke of all, for I felt certain that I should never return.

I went back to my bunk and sweated and shivered with fear. My mind and my body seemed to be completely separated from each other, and I found it quite impossible to stop the quaking of my limbs. I saw Death in a thousand forms just as on the night before the attack at Courtrai. Sleep was impossible, so I

RAILWAY TROOPS WITH THE AMMUNITION TRAIN

RAILWAY TROOPS

got up at last and wrote these lines with a trembling hand. The others are chipping me about "My Last Will and Testament," and there is the usual fatuous talk of medals. Day says that if I come back, they will roll all my previous non-fructifying recommendations into one and make it a real V.C. at last. Oh! God, if they only knew—and they look to me as a sort of Bayard.—*Written at Calais waiting for leave boat.*

After leaving the mess and that infernal warrant, I calmed down somewhat and was able to get my mind on to the work ahead—my old campaigning instincts began to return and I became once more a scout, clear-headed and fearless. It was a grand night for my work, miserable and stormy, with rain and hail blowing in the gusty wind. Arrived in the outposts it dawned on me that Stephens would be quite useless, and I couldn't remember why I had ever decided to take him—if things went all right, he could do nothing, and if they found us it would be two corpses instead of one. He pleaded to come with me, and I had to hurt his feelings to get rid of him.

I got all the information I could from the outpost officers, said goodbye to them, and went forward towards the river. It was then about half a mile in front of me, and separated from our posts by a belt of marsh and flooded fields. This belt was traversed by two roads with a small bridge in each where they crossed a stream running parallel to the main river. I had to investigate these two roads and bridges and the main bridge where the two roads joined across the river. It was my plan to work up one road, look at the river, and the main bridge, and then return down the other road.

There was practically no cover on the road, but the night was dark and I felt fairly safe along the water's edge. I calculated that I had gone 200 yards and then I waited, as I was a little nervous at having heard nothing, and felt certain that there would be posts along the road. After five minutes I heard the tapping of a mallet on stakes, and knew that they were wiring some 200 yards down the road. Still I waited, but I had no clear notion why. I assumed, of course, that there were protective troops on this side of the wiring party, but it was instinct rather than reason which made me halt.

I was just preparing to go forward again when two men rose out of the road not 15 yards away, walked a few paces up and down the road, and then appeared to lie down again. I had all but walked on to their rifles and my heart thumped crazily. There was nothing for it but to take to the water and the marsh. I retreated 20 yards and waded in, holding my revolver over my head. It was deathly cold, and after about 100 yards I nearly gave it up—at times the water was up to my shoulders and I seemed to make no progress. The noise of the working party guided me, and eventually I judged that I was behind them and therefore about in line with the first small bridge.

About this time, I realised that another five minutes in the water would kill me, and I struck back for the road, regardless of everything except a desire to get on dry land. Unfortunately, I blundered into a colony of waterfowl, and they flew up all round my head, making a terrific noise. My heart stood still and I waited again—was there a scout among those Huns on the road, who could read the meaning of the terrified waterfowl?

Apparently not, for I still heard the regular tapping of the mallets, and several minutes later I was lying exhausted by the roadside. I half emptied my flask and pushed on up the road—I was right in the middle of the Huns now and crawling on my stomach as I did not know how near or far they might be—I thought the cold would kill me, and wondered what the Huns would think to find a dead Englishman inside their lines.

To my unspeakable delight there was no one on the bridge, and I was able to make a thorough examination. I laughed at the Huns working solemnly down the road, and for a second forgot my terrible condition. Here I think my mind went a little dull, as I blundered straight on down the road until I had almost reached the river and the main bridge. It was sheer madness, but I would certainly have perished without the movement to aid my circulation. I remember thinking grimly that it would be just my fate to die of a cold after all that I had been through. I found a lot of Huns round the bridge, so I struck the river about yards above it and then worked down under cover of the banks.

I spent some twenty minutes under the bridge and all the time I could hear their voices in the darkness above me—the meaning of their words was drowned by the noise of the wind and the rain. Now I had to get back down the other road before it began to grow light, and, as I truly imagined, deliver my message before I died. Half a mile inside the Hun lines, after spending two hours up to my shoulders in water on a November night my condition is better imagined than described.

I ate a sodden mass of crumbs and bully that had once been sandwiches in my pocket and finished the rum. I was nearly caught in getting to the downstream side of the bridge and lay shivering under a hedge for several minutes while a party marched by within three paces of my head. I think they were the working party off the road and I noticed that it was beginning to grow lighter luckily the storm grew worse.

Eventually I got on to the second road and crawled back along the water's edge until I came to my last bridge—there was a German machine-gun party sitting right in the middle of it. My brain was still perfect, but I had lost all sense of feeling in my body—I wanted to cry—they sat there between me and England, and I believe I had some idea of getting up and asking them to let me go home. For a few minutes I had no more will-power than a child. Then some of our shells came over and I could hear them bursting on the road over the bridge. There was only one way back and that was as I had come—through the water. I forgot all about the stream and waded in.

The cold seemed to pull me together, although, God knows, nothing could be colder than my own body. There was a bit of dry land between the flood and the stream, but I got across without being seen—I was keeping close to the bridge in the hope of seeing something of it as I passed. If I couldn't wade the stream I was done, but I determined to try even if my head was under water and I had to hold my breath. It was not more than five feet deep in the centre and I got across and so over the bank into the flood on the far side. I had still to keep to the water, as I was afraid there would be a patrol on the road in advance of the people on the bridge.

A few of our shells were still falling on the road, and I could hear the angry hisses as the red-hot bits of steel rained into the water round about. I did about 200 yards like this and then I gave up—it was either the road or collapse and drowning in the water. I got on to the road, worked back carefully until I felt safe, and then ran like the devil until I knew I was inside our posts. When I stopped I nearly fainted, so I set off again—my head pulling me up into the clouds like a bubble and my legs holding me to the road as if they were tons of lead.

Eventually I came across some gunners and they marvelled at the whisky I drank. I told them I had been out scouting and slipped into some water—I didn't really know what had happened just at the time—I had vague impressions of a mass of water and some Germans sitting on a bridge, refusing to let me go home. Then I fell asleep, just sat down bang on the mess floor and collapsed.

They woke me after a couple of hours, lent me a horse, and directed me to the company.

Tomorrow I shall be in England.

*Nov. 9.* In the paper this morning there is a brief announcement that the Second Army is across the Scheldt. I was proud to see it and felt amply rewarded for my terrible night in the water. It has left no apparent after-effects, so there must have been more resistance left in my old carcass than I gave myself credit for.

*Nov. 11.* It is over. These last few days I have hardly dared to hope for it, and now that it has come, I can hardly realise exactly what it means. The thought of going back to it was killing me, and I have been suffering from the most ghastly nightmare dreams—sometimes I am stuck in the wire, unable to duck, with bullets whistling past my head—another time I am trying to run through knee-deep mud with the shell-bursts slowly overtaking me. I haven't slept peacefully since my return, but think it will be better now.

I went out to see the celebrations tonight, and had only one regret—that my revolver was left in Flanders.

*For of these how many know,*
*Or, how many knowing, care*
*Of the things that bought them this*
*In the mud fields over there.*
*It is most emphatically forthwith be forgotten.*
*over and will*

Stockholm, Sweden,<br>30th Aug., 1920.

It is late at night and I am lying on the silken cushions of a private yacht; my host's daughter, a beautiful blue-eyed girl, is reclining by my side, her hand on my shoulder.

All around us the harbour lights are twinkling merrily and the warm breath of the idle breeze carries the sound of pleasant music from the gardens in the town. The little waves whisper and sigh seductively under the stem of the ship, and overhead, "the sort, lascivious stars leer from the velvet skies." I recall a similar night at Colwyn in 1914 and wonder if these people, too, will fail to read the writing on the wall.

We are living once more in the days of "pomp and cir-cumstance"—each morning I see their Guards march to the Royal Palace with brazen music and all the childish pageantry of war—each afternoon I see their sartorially perfect officers parade the Strandvagen before the gay-gowned beauties of the *cafés*.

Is there no one with the courage to tell them that war is not like this, that there will come a day without music, when there are no bright colours and no admiring eyes, but when "the lice are in their hair and the scabs are on their tongue"? Surely our years of sacrifice were vain if the most highly educated people in Europe remain in ig-norance of the real nature of war and are open scoffers at the League of Nations. They believe that England is the biggest brigand in the world, and look upon Germany as the home of all Progress, valiantly defending herself against a league of jealous enemies. To me it is incredible and I remonstrate—they mention Ireland, Egypt, India,

THE WORCESTSHIRE REGIMENT

and Versailles.

Then I realise that the bitterest passages in my diary are only too true—the sway of the old men has returned, the dead are forgotten, and betrayed. Please God that they may never know the futility of their sacrifice.

I am weary and tired of life myself; a mere shell of a man, without health or strength, whose vitality was eaten out by the Flanders mud. This ease and luxury is sent to mock me; I fling my cigar overboard with angry contempt.

Along the northern sky the summer sunset is mingling with the dawn in a riot of impossible colours. My mind turns back to a day when Gheluvelt lay smoking in the sun, England still slumbered, and the flower of the Prussian Army were pouring in overwhelming numbers along the road to Calais. The 1st Division was fought to a standstill, dying in thousands but yielding not an inch; the 7th was practically annihilated but somehow held their line, counterattacking again and again until the khaki drops were swallowed in the sea of grey; there was an open gap at last. Haig himself rode down the Menin road to call for a last effort from the weary men; a gunner officer, his arm hanging in shreds from the shoulder, took his last gun on to the open road and fired into the grey masses until he died; the Worcesters flung their remnants across the road, and the line was made again. The whitest gentlemen of England died that day, and I would that I had rotted in their company before I saw their sacred trust betrayed. We have dropped their fiery torch and the silken cushions call us.

LEONAUR

# ALSO FROM LEONAUR
## AVAILABLE IN SOFTCOVER OR HARDCOVER WITH DUST JACKET

**ESCAPE FROM THE FRENCH** *by Edward Boys*—A Young Royal Navy Midshipman's Adventures During the Napoleonic War.

**THE VOYAGE OF H.M.S. PANDORA** *by Edward Edwards R. N. & George Hamilton, edited by Basil Thomson*—In Pursuit of the Mutineers of the Bounty in the South Seas—1790-1791.

**MEDUSA** *by J. B. Henry Savigny and Alexander Correard and Charlotte-Adélaïde Dard* —Narrative of a Voyage to Senegal in 1816 & The Sufferings of the Picard Family After the Shipwreck of the Medusa.

**THE SEA WAR OF 1812 VOLUME 1** *by A. T. Mahan*—A History of the Maritime Conflict.

**THE SEA WAR OF 1812 VOLUME 2** *by A. T. Mahan*—A History of the Maritime Conflict.

**WETHERELL OF H. M. S. HUSSAR** *by John Wetherell*—The Recollections of an Ordinary Seaman of the Royal Navy During the Napoleonic Wars.

**THE NAVAL BRIGADE IN NATAL** *by C. R. N. Burne*—With the Guns of H. M. S. Terrible & H. M. S. Tartar during the Boer War 1899-1900.

**THE VOYAGE OF H. M. S. BOUNTY** *by William Bligh*—The True Story of an 18th Century Voyage of Exploration and Mutiny.

**SHIPWRECK!** *by William Gilly*—The Royal Navy's Disasters at Sea 1793-1849.

**KING'S CUTTERS AND SMUGGLERS: 1700-1855** *by E. Keble Chatterton*—A unique period of maritime history-from the beginning of the eighteenth to the middle of the nineteenth century when British seamen risked all to smuggle valuable goods from wool to tea and spirits from and to the Continent.

**CONFEDERATE BLOCKADE RUNNER** *by John Wilkinson*—The Personal Recollections of an Officer of the Confederate Navy.

**NAVAL BATTLES OF THE NAPOLEONIC WARS** *by W. H. Fitchett*—Cape St. Vincent, the Nile, Cadiz, Copenhagen, Trafalgar & Others.

**PRISONERS OF THE RED DESERT** *by R. S. Gwatkin-Williams*—The Adventures of the Crew of the Tara During the First World War.

**U-BOAT WAR 1914-1918** *by James B. Connolly/Karl von Schenk*—Two Contrasting Accounts from Both Sides of the Conflict at Sea D uring the Great War.